HE SHALL BE CALLED

He SHALL BE CALLED

150 NAMES OF JESUS AND WHAT THEY MEAN TO YOU

ROBERT J. MORGAN

WARNER
Faith®

New York   Boston   Nashville

To Joshua and Grace

Warner Faith

Time Warner Book Group
1271 Avenue of the Americas, New York, NY 10020
Visit our Web site at www.twbookmark.com

The Warner Faith name and logo are registered trademarks of Time Warner Book Group Inc.

Printed in the United States of America
First Warner Faith printing: October 2005
10 9 8 7 6 5 4 3 2 1

Library of Congress Cataloging-in-Publication Data
Morgan, Robert J.
    He shall be called : 150 names of Jesus and what they mean to you / Robert J. Morgan.
        p. cm.
    Includes bibliographical references.
    ISBN 0-446-57652-2
    1. Jesus Christ—Name. 2. Success—Religious aspects—Christianity. I. Title.
    BT590.N2M63 2005
    232—dc22   2005014720

ACKNOWLEDGMENTS

Consider this an engraved invitation to spend some pleasant days getting to know Jesus Christ through His manifold and marvelous names. God is in the habit of blessing those who study His name, for Psalm 119:132 says: "Look upon me and be merciful to me, / As Your custom is toward those who love Your name."

Something remarkable happens as we learn about the names of our Lord Jesus. We come to know Him better, and, in the process, we develop greater joy and deeper faith. Psalm 5:11 says: "Let those also who love Your name / Be joyful in you." And Psalm 9:10 says, "Those who know Your name will put their trust in You."

In these pages you'll find 260 Scriptural names, titles, and descriptive phrases for Jesus. Along with my own comments, I've included some classic quotes from earlier centuries, especially from the incredible sermons of the Prince of Preachers, Charles Haddon Spurgeon, which I've taken the liberty to update slightly and condense. When he was seventeen years old, Spurgeon was asked to pastor a small congregation in Waterbeach village. His first sermon there was to a dozen people. Soon hundreds were attending each week, and the doors and windows of the church were left open so the overflow could hear. Two years later, he moved to London. Despite his youthful appearance, he set the city afire, packing London's greatest auditoriums and preaching to thousands without aid of microphone or amplification.

I like Spurgeon's sermons so much better than his writings. He himself once admitted that writing was difficult for him, but his sermons poured from his mouth in remarkable bursts of seemingly spontaneous oratory. He used no pulpit, and he preached his eloquent discourses with only a few notes on a table beside him as he stood at the platform railing.

In addition to my own Spurgeon resources, I am indebted to www.spurgeon.org for its excellent and growing archives. I'm also thankful to www.cyberhymnal.org, one of my favorite Internet sites, for its fantastic research into Christian hymnody. I have included a verse from an old hymn with every devotional. The handful of unattributed verses is my own.

This book wouldn't have been possible without the help of some dear friends. Sincere thanks go to Greg Johnson who encouraged the idea from the beginning and to Lee Hough for his guidance and support.

My literary agent, Chris Ferebee of Yates and Yates, has been a great encouragement. Special thanks to my editor, Leslie Peterson, whose friendliness, vision, and competence have been invaluable.

I also want to thank my sister, Ann Campbell, for running our childhood home, Roan Mountain Bed and Breakfast, in my absence, and for keeping a room ready for me whenever I needed to hole away.

My personal secretary, Sherry Anderson, keeps my life on schedule, and I thank her for that. And I thank each of you for picking up this book. If you'd like to get in touch with me, please do so at www.robertjmorgan.com.

Most of all, I love and appreciate my wife, Katrina, who read every word of this manuscript—and changed quite a few of them, and all for the better.

CONTENTS

Contents

I know my words cannot honor Him according to His merits: I wish they could. Indeed, I grow less and less satisfied with my thoughts and language concerning Him. He is too glorious for my feeble language to describe Him. If I could speak with the tongues of men and of angels, I could not speak worthily of Him. If I could borrow all the harmonies of heaven, and enlist every harp and song of the glorified, yet were not the music sweet enough for His praises. Our glorious Redeemer is ever blessed: let us bless Him.

—CHARLES HADDON SPURGEON
FEBRUARY 16, 1881

PREFACE

If you could choose your own name, what would it be? Do you see yourself as a Britney, Bernardo, Shaquille, or Sam? What about Claudia, Carla, Arlo, or Alfonso?

My name is Robert, but one of my regrets is that I never asked my parents why they chose that name. There are no other known Roberts in my family tree, and its meaning—"bright fame"—hardly describes a hillbilly boy like me from the Tennessee mountains. I might have called myself John, after my dad, or Jim, or George.

So what's your name? Where does it come from? Does it have special meaning or significance? Is it descriptive of your personality or character? Do you like it, or would you prefer another?

Such questions belong to the area of onomastics, a term coming from the Greek word *onoma,* meaning "name." Onomastics is the study of names, and an *onomastikan* is a list of names. A vast body of literature exists on this subject, and such organizations as the American Name Society, founded in 1951, promote the study of onomastics. From these sources we learn that our names have one primary purpose: to distinguish us from other people and to give us our own identity.

As it turns out, names are very interesting. All of us have monikers that in one way or another have meaningful origins. Take our English surnames as an example. Experts tell us the majority of them developed from one of four different criteria:

1. Some are based on locality. The name Appleby, for example, means "By the apple tree." I know a family named Woods. Where do you think their ancestors lived? I have another friend named West. At some time or another, his forbearers must have lived west of a town somewhere, or perhaps west of the Woods.

2. Other names come from one's occupation. If a man named Thomas was a cook, he became known as Thomas the Cook, or Thomas Cook. Same for Baker, Farmer, Smith,

and Taylor. I know a man named Bowman, one of whose ancestors was evidentially a skilled archer.

3. A third category of surnames originated from the given name of a father. If a man named John was the son of a John, then he would be John John's son, or John Johnson.

4. A fourth category developed from personal characteristics. James Strong, the man who compiled a famous concordance, must have had a very muscular ancestor. Henry Wadsworth Longfellow had a tall fellow somewhere in his family tree. When I was growing up, the Little family lived on one side of town, and the Stouts on the other (though strangely the Stouts were little and the Littles were stout).

Perhaps your mind is racing to figure out the etymology of your own name. I did a bit of checking on my surname, Morgan, and found it fit into the first category; it was a locality-based name. It appears to have come from the old Welsh word, *mor,* meaning "moor" or "sea." The suffix *gan* may have meant "born." If so, I could infer that somewhere in my ancestry I had a forefather who was born on the high seas. It is essentially the same as the name Seaborne.

So far I've been talking about English names, but experts tell us that remarkable similarities exist in almost every culture, including African, Latin, and Asian ones. These patterns do not greatly vary from land to land.

It was especially true in the society of the ancient Hebrews, for they took seriously the naming of a child. They didn't give their kids names that were trendy or that merely sounded good. They wanted their children to wear meaningful monikers.

Samuel is a good example. His mother, Hannah, was a woman distraught by infertility who begged God for a child. The Bible says, "So it came to pass in the process of time that Hannah conceived and bore a son, and called his name Samuel, saying, 'Because I have asked for him from the LORD'" (1 Sam. 1:20).

The prefix *Sam* is related to the Hebrew verb meaning "to hear," and the *el* at the end is a Hebrew word for God. His name meant: "God Heard!" Samuel was named, as it were, "Answered Prayer."

In the Bible, then, a person's name was not just his or her identification, but his or her description.

With that in mind, it shouldn't surprise us that the greatest man in the Bible—the Source and Center of the Scriptures, the Peerless Personage around whom the Bible revolves—would have not just one name, or two, or three, but scores and scores of names, for He Himself is indescribable.

Some time ago, I decided to read leisurely from Genesis to Revelation, noting every name, title, and descriptive phrase that identifies Christ. I found about 350, and I'm sure I missed some along the way.

Why so many names and titles for our Lord Jesus Christ? Because He is so infinite, so vast, so multidimensioned and poly-faceted. It takes all these names to describe Him, just as it would take all the colors of the spectrum to adequately paint His portrait.

Since all His attributes are infinite and limitless, Jesus of Nazareth can no more be contained in His names and titles than the atmosphere can be captured in a series of oxygen tanks, or the ocean bottled in a collection of containers however beautiful. He is timeless and boundless, and His infinity extends through the universe into endless, perpetual depths of forever-ness.

Yet He reveals Himself through His designations, and all His glorious names meet varying needs in our own lives. They reveal diverse dimensions of His power, love, grace, glory, and goodness that touch our souls. They disclose the many layers of His relationship with us. His names help us fix our thoughts on Him in new ways. They fill our minds with Him who can fill our hearts and guide our lives. Each of His names helps us comprehend and appreciate Him as we should, and they reassure us of His love in so many different ways.

This is not a study on the names of God the Father or God the Spirit, as I have not included names and titles such as Jehovah or Holy Ghost. It's limited to the names and titles of God the Son, the second person of the Trinity. Even then, as I indicated, it isn't an exhaustive list. I could easily pick up my Bible this afternoon and find a name or title I've never noticed before. Jesus is on every page of Scripture, and His glorious names are scattered thither and yon throughout both Old and New Testaments.

For the sake of an orderly arrangement, I've classified the names under different headings, but these are not watertight compartments. Some of His names could aptly be placed in more than one category. I've tried to explain the meaning of each name and to show how it relates to us. Our Lord's names and titles are so rich they must be pondered, savored, mulled over, and thoughtfully applied to the heart. His love is spread across our souls, His promises are under our feet, His presence is around our lives, and His name is above every name.

HE SHALL BE CALLED

JESUS

A Man called Jesus.

—JOHN 9:11

ONCE WHEN I FLEW INTO SAN FRANCISCO FOR A SPEAKING engagement, a man picked me up at the airport and took me to a restaurant on the coast. He was alert, sharply dressed, and excited about the Lord. He seemed to have boundless energy, and his eyes sparkled. Over lunch, he handed me an old snapshot. "Do you recognize this man?" he asked.

I studied the photograph but drew a blank. The man in the picture was old and weary. His stringy hair was matted, his eyes glazed over, his skin blotched and unhealthy. Handing the picture back, I shook my head. "It doesn't ring a bell," I said. "Is he someone I should know?"

"It's me," he said, smiling. "This is my *before* picture. This is what I was like before I met Jesus as my Savior."

It was a welcome reminder to me that Jesus saves. He salvages. He restores and renovates us. And His mission is bound up in His name.

From one perspective, there was nothing unusual about the name *Jesus*. It was a common designation in the biblical world, and many Jewish parents called their boys Jesus, up until the second century. In some cultures, it's still popular. The Bible records four other men named *Jesus* (see Col. 4:11, for example). This name therefore speaks of His humanity, His ordinariness.

But it also speaks of His *extra*ordinariness. *Jesus* is the New Testament version of the Old Testament name *Joshua,* and it comes from two shorter Hebrew words—the name *Jehovah* coupled with the verb *to save.* Literally, "Jehovah Saves" or "Jehovah Delivers."

That explains the angel's message to Joseph: "You shall call His name JESUS [Jehovah Saves], for He will save His people from their sins" (Matt. 1:21). This name embodies His mission and conveys His purpose: to seek and to save those who are lost, to seek and to save people like my friend in San Francisco, and people like you and me.

Jesus! Name of wondrous love,
Human name of God above!
Pleading only this, we flee,
Helpless, O our God, to Thee.

—WILLIAM W. HOW, 1854

YESHUA/JOSHUA

This is the genealogy of Yeshua the Messiah, son of David.

—MATTHEW 1:1 (THE JEWISH NEW TESTAMENT)

YESHUA WAS WHAT THEY CALLED HIM. THAT'S HOW THEY SAID it, how the syllables sounded as they drifted through the carpenter's cottage or across the Nazarene hillsides. We say *Joshua* in English, but the Hebrew form is *Yeshua* and the Greek form is *Iesous,* from which we get our English pronunciation "Jesus."

Jesus, Joshua, Yeshua, and *Iesous* are all one and the same name, pronounced slightly differently depending on the language.

Simply put, the angel of the Lord directed Joseph and Mary to name their little boy after the great Old Testament general, Joshua, who led the Israelites into the promised land.

In Numbers 13, Moses selected twelve men to explore the land of Canaan in preparation for the Israeli invasion. One was Hoshea, son of Nun. Verse 16 says: "And Moses called Hoshea son of Nun, Joshua." Moses changed the man's name. Why?

Most commentators are mystified. The two names are similar. *Hoshea* means "May Jehovah Save," and *Joshua* means "Jehovah Is Salvation." But it seems to me that Moses was led by God to strengthen Hoshea's name to make it more solid, more durable, more certain, more dogmatic. Why? Because it would later belong to one greater than Joshua.

The two men, after all, shared a similar task. Joshua followed Moses the Lawgiver and led the people into the future God had planned for them. After the death of Moses, Joshua rose up to do what Moses could not do: lead the Israelites across the Jordan River into victory.

The New Testament Joshua came to do what the Law itself could not do and to lead us into eternal life. Romans 8:3–4 says, "For what the law could not do in that it was weak through the flesh, God did by sending His own Son in the likeness of sinful flesh, on account of sin: He condemned sin in the flesh, that the righteous requirement of the law might be fulfilled in us who do not walk according to the flesh but according to the Spirit."

Jehovah is salvation!

*How sweet the Name of Jesus sounds
In a believer's ear!
It soothes his sorrows, heals his wounds,
And drives away his fear.*

—JOHN NEWTON, 1779

JESUS OF NAZARETH

So they told him that Jesus of Nazareth was passing by.
—LUKE 18:37

HAVE YOU KNOWN THE PAIN OF PARTING? GREAT SORROW comes with separation, whether caused by death, distance, divorce, or disagreement. I remember the tears I shed when I left for college, and the ones I shed years later when my own children grew up and left home.

After being elected president, Abraham Lincoln stood at the railroad station in Springfield, Illinois, to bid farewell to home and family. He said:

> *My friends, no one . . . can appreciate my feelings of sadness at this parting. To this place, and the kindness of these people, I owe everything. Here I have lived a quarter of a century, and have passed from a young to an old man. Here my children have been born, and one is buried. I now leave, not knowing when, or whether ever, I may return.*

Jesus must have felt that way when leaving Nazareth. Today, Nazareth is a largely Arab town of sixty thousand, but in our Lord's day it was a Jewish village nestled on a hillside in the lower Galilee. This was the home of Joseph and Mary. There Jesus spent His early years before leaving to assume His ministry.

I wonder if His heart broke as He hung up his carpenter's apron for the last time, packed a few essentials, said His good-byes, and left Nazareth to march toward Calvary. I wonder if He turned for a last, poignant glance at the happy haunts of His childhood in "Nazareth, where He had been brought up" (Luke 4:16).

But then, He was used to such sadness. He had left home once before. I wonder if, on that previous occasion, He had turned for a final poignant look at the ivory palaces of heaven before leaving home to save the world.

Since He knows the sorrow of separation, He can comfort us in our sorrows and separations. After all, who or what can separate us from the love of Christ? "Neither death nor life, nor angels nor principalities nor powers, nor things present nor things to come, nor height nor depth, nor any other created thing, shall be able to separate us from the love of God which is in Christ Jesus our Lord" (Rom. 8:35–39).

Who is this Jesus? Why should He
The city move so mightily?
A passing stranger, has He skill
To move the multitude at will?
Again the stirring tones reply,
"Jesus of Nazareth passeth by."

—EMMA CAMPBELL, 1863

THE NAZARENE

He shall be called a Nazarene.

—MATTHEW 2:23

JESUS UNDOUBTEDLY DEVELOPED GOOD LEG MUSCLES AS A boy, for the town of Nazareth sat on a fairly steep hillside, and any little trip required going up and down the slopes. His arms were rock solid, too, for the only water supply was a spring at the bottom of the hill, and one of His chores was certainly to haul water from the spring.

It was this spring, in fact, that kept Nazareth from becoming a large city. No other reliable sources of water existed, so the entire town depended on the one spring. Today it's called Mary's Well, and it still provides water for Nazareth. According to old traditions, it was by this spring that Gabriel gave Mary the news that would change her world, and ours.

How odd that God chose Nazareth for our Lord's upbringing. How unexpected. From an obscure village came the central figure of history. From small-town Israel came the Savior of the masses. How strange that for thirty years, a simple spring quenched the thirst of Him who would be called the Water of Life, that a small carpenter's shop would be home to the Builder of the universe.

Don't ever feel limited by your background. Perhaps you were born with few advantages. Maybe in a small town. Maybe in a dysfunctional home. Maybe with an inborn difficulty. Maybe you were ridiculed, abused, or injured in earlier years. Can any good come out of that? Jesus can make it so.

Sometimes our disadvantages and weaknesses become the very things God uses to bless us and to make us a blessing to others. The Nazarene knows how to use your background—whatever it is—for His eternal purposes. Leave your background in the background, trusting Him to work all things together for good, and press on toward what lies ahead.

I stand amazed in the presence
Of Jesus the Nazarene,
And wonder how He could love me,
A sinner, condemned, unclean.
O how marvelous! O how wonderful!
And my song shall ever be:
O how marvelous! O how wonderful!
Is my Savior's love for me!

—CHARLES H. GABRIEL, 1905

THE GALILEAN

Now Peter was sitting outside in the courtyard, and a servant-girl came to him and said, "You too were with Jesus the Galilean."

—Matthew 26:69 (NASB)

GALILEE IS A LAND OF LIMESTONE HILLS, FERTILE PLAINS, quaint villages, and small cities, watered by dependable springs. There the Jordan begins its descent through Israel, pausing midstream to form the Sea of Galilee. The Israelis have a saying: "God made the seven seas for the world but reserved the Sea of Galilee for Himself." If there was ever a land rich with God's blessings, it was Galilee.

Yet after the death of King Solomon, Galilee revolted and formed a rebel nation. Rejecting Jehovah as their God, these northern tribes began worshiping a golden calf. They sank deeply into idolatry and sin, creating massive problems for themselves on many levels: morally, politically, spiritually, and economically.

Finally, in 734 BC, the brutal Assyrian king, Tiglath-pilesar III, swept them away. A mixture of Gentiles took possession. The land became known as Galilee of the Gentiles and appeared lost to the Jewish people; their iniquities had brought destruction on their own heads.

But God is a God of remarkable grace. During the darkest days of the Northern Kingdom, Isaiah predicted that the Lord wasn't finished with Galilee. He would yet do something remarkable with this land of verdant hills and sparkling waters. From Galilee would come a Messiah with light for the world. "In the future," wrote Isaiah,

He will honor Galilee of the Gentiles, by the way of the sea, along the Jordan—

> *The people walking in darkness*
> *have seen a great light;*

on those living in the land of the shadow of death
a light has dawned. (9:1–2)

Against all odds, it happened as Isaiah predicted. It was in Galilean Nazareth that Jesus grew up. Nearby was Capernaum, headquarters of our Lord's earthly ministry. His Sermon on the Mount, His transfiguration, and most of His parables and miracles occurred in Galilee.

Many of us, like Nazareth, have squandered our blessings by foolish choices and outright rebellion. But we have a God who can restore messed-up lives, heal chronic hurts, make up for lost days, and bring good out of evil.

Trust His surprising grace.

Hail, Thou once despisèd Jesus! Hail, Thou Galilean King!
Thou didst suffer to release us; Thou didst free salvation bring.
Hail, Thou universal Savior, Who hast borne our sin and shame!
By Thy merits we find favor; life is given through Thy Name.

—JOHN BAKEWELL, 1757

$\mathscr{I}$MMANUEL/GOD WITH US

"They shall call His name Immanuel," which is translated,
"God with us."

—MATTHEW 1:23

RECENTLY A FRIEND WROTE TO ME ABOUT HIS SINGLENESS,
saying,

> *I'm more or less content alone, I suppose. I've had so many adventures*
> *in my life already; I'm used to doing them alone. But there's this sense*
> *of lacking. It fades in and out. It's always waiting in the background*
> *for a weak moment. I've prayed many times for someone to share*
> *these adventures with, but the Lord's time hasn't come yet.*

Are you lonely? Fellowship with God, however rich, cannot re-
place companionship with another person, as Adam discovered in
Genesis 2:18 when God said, "It is not good that man should be alone;
I will make him a helper comparable to him."

No, but the Lord's camaraderie goes a long way in filling up the
void. Learning to practice the presence of God is a vital art in victorious Christian living. His name is: God with Us!

For centuries, poets and hymnists have marveled at the wonder of
God's downward journey to live among us. No greater theme has
ever been found; no greater truth can be sung. God is with us! He is
with you!

Paul Gerhardt, one of my favorite hymnists, was a student in Wit-
tenberg, Germany, and later a pastor in Berlin. As a youth, he had endured the Thirty Years' War and the ensuing plague. "What has my
whole existence been since my youth other than difficulty and misery?" he once wrote. "As long as I can remember I have spent some
mornings and some nights with problems and concerns upon my
heart."[1]

But God was with him, giving daily vigor and victory. Gerhardt put it this way in his beautiful Christmas carol, "Wir singen dir, Immanuel," written in 1653:

We sing, Immanuel, Thy praise,
Thou Prince of life and Fount of grace,
Thou Flower of heaven and Star of morn,
Thou Lord of lords, Thou virgin born.
Hallelujah!

And I, Thy servant, Lord, today
Confess my love and freely say,
I love Thee truly, but I would
That I might love Thee as I should.
Hallelujah!

—PAUL GERHARDT, 1653

$\mathscr{A}$ BABE

You will find a Babe wrapped in swaddling cloths, lying in a manger.

—LUKE 2:12

WHY SHEPHERDS? WHY DIDN'T THE ANGELS APPEAR TO, well, rabbis or some other group in the holy hush of that first Christmas night? Why didn't they announce Messiah's birth to the leaders of Israel? Why specifically to shepherds? I have three ideas about it.

First, Jesus came to the poor. The appearance of the angels to the shepherds is the perfect complement to His being born in a stable and laid in a manger. It symbolized His poverty. He had left the ivory palaces of heaven to come into a world of woe. He who had been rich became poor that we through His poverty might become rich. Alexander Maclaren said, "The appearance to these humble men as they sat simply chatting in a rustic row symbolizes the destination of the Gospel for all ranks and classes."

Second, Jesus was the long-awaited heir of David's throne. And who was David? He was the shepherd-king who had once kept flocks in those very fields. It was to a new generation of shepherds, to the vocational descendants of the ancient shepherd-king, that angels made the announcement as to the birth of another Shepherd who would become King of the Jews.

Third, it was a Lamb being born that night. The picture of a Lamb is the Bible's most consistent type of Christ. In the book of Exodus, the Passover lamb was slain and its blood painted across the doorposts of the homes of the Israelites, and the Lord said, "When I see the blood I will pass over you," referring to the angel of judgment. The prophet Isaiah wrote, "He was led as a lamb to the slaughter, / And as a sheep before its shearers is silent, / So He opened not His mouth." When John the Baptist came introducing Christ to the masses, he used these words: "Behold! The Lamb of God who takes away the sin of the world!" (Exod. 12:13; Isa. 53:7; John 1:29).

Furthermore, the Hebrew scholar Alfred Edersheim tells us that the flocks near Bethlehem were no ordinary sheep; they were being raised for sacrificial use in the temple. As Ruth Graham said, "How right the angels should appear to them that night."

Thank God for His coming as a babe, and for all it means to us.

I know not how that Bethlehem's Babe
Could in the Godhead be;
I only know the manger Child
Has brought God's life to me.

—HARRY W. FARRINGTON, 1910

THAT WHICH IS CONCEIVED IN HER

Joseph, son of David, do not be afraid to take to you Mary your wife, for that which is conceived in her is of the Holy Spirit.

—MATTHEW 1:20

SHORTLY AFTER I YIELDED MY LIFE TO JESUS CHRIST AS A college sophomore, a friend of mine in the dormitory begin meeting with me each week to teach me the Bible. One day he asked, "Rob, if someone asked you to explain simply and plainly who Jesus Christ was, what would you say? Who is He?"

"He's the Lord," I replied.

"No," said Joe, "that's His title. It tells us what He does; He rules over all creation. But as a person, who is He?"

"He's my Savior," I said.

"No," said my friend, "that tells us what He did on the cross, but exactly who is He?"

I tried several other answers, but Joe struck them all down. Then he smiled and said, "I can answer the question in two words: He's the God-Man. He is absolutely, utterly, and completely God, and He is absolutely, utterly, and completely human. It isn't that He's fifty-fifty, half-God, half-man. He is totally God and totally man. He has always been God and always will be God. But He became a man at Bethlehem, and from the moment of His conception in the virgin's womb, He has been, is, and always will be human. When we see Him in eternity, He will still be the God-Man."

Joe went on to explain, "He had to be God in order to save us, for only God is pure and powerful enough to forgive our sins and give eternal life. Isaiah 43:11 says, 'I, even I, am the LORD, / And besides Me there is no Savior.' But He had to be a man in order to die to provide that salvation. Hence, the genius of God, that Jesus Christ was made both fully human and fully divine."

That conversation took place over thirty years ago, but I've never forgotten it. I realize now that it explains one of the deepest mysteries about the life of Christ: His virgin birth. The Holy Spirit "overshadowed" Mary (Luke 1:35), and she was found to be pregnant "of the Holy Spirit." Jesus, therefore, was both human and divine, both God and man.

That makes Him unique in history, peerless in the universe, and matchless in my life.

Come, and Christ the Lord be praising,
Heart and mind to Him be raising,
Celebrate His love amazing,
Worthy folk of Christendom.

—PAUL GERHARDT, 1667

THE CHILD JESUS

And when the parents brought in the Child Jesus . . .

—LUKE 2:27

ONCE AS I WAS READING THROUGH THE NATIVITY ACCOUNT of Luke 1 and 2, I noticed something I hadn't seen before. Seven distinct people or groups celebrated that first Christmas, and they all responded the same way.

First there was Elizabeth, Mary's relative, in Luke 1: "And Elizabeth was filled with the Holy Spirit. Then she spoke out with a loud voice and said, 'Blessed are you among women, and blessed is the fruit of your womb!'" (vv. 41–42).

Mary responded: "My soul magnifies the Lord, / And my spirit has rejoiced in God my Savior" (vv. 46–47).

Zacharias, finally getting into the Christmas spirit, said: "Blessed is the Lord God of Israel, / For He has visited and redeemed His people" (v. 68).

In Luke 2, we see the exuberance of the angels who were singing: "Glory to God in the highest, / And on earth peace, goodwill toward men!" (v. 14).

In response, the shepherds rushed into town and saw the Christ child. Luke 2:20 says, "Then the shepherds returned, glorifying and praising God."

Later, when Mary and Joseph took Jesus to Jerusalem to present him to the Lord, they met two important figures, an old man named Simeon and an aged woman named Anna. Taking the Christ child in his arms, Simeon blessed God, saying: "Lord, now You are letting Your servant depart in peace, / According to Your word" (Luke 20:29).

Anna, "coming in that instant, . . . gave thanks to the Lord, and spoke of Him to all those who looked for the redemption in Israel" (Luke 2:38).

His Nativity Names

In my journal, I made note of this:

1. Elizabeth, filled with the Spirit, cried out with a loud voice.

2. Mary said: "My soul magnifies the Lord."

3. Zacharias said: "Blessed is the Lord God of Israel."

4. The angels said: "Glory to God in the highest."

5. The shepherds "returned, glorifying and praising God."

6. Simeon held the child in his arms and blessed God.

7. Anna gave thanks to the Lord and spoke of Him.

How, then, should we celebrate Christmas this year?

All praise to Thee, Eternal Lord,
Clothed in a garb of flesh and blood;
Choosing a manger for Thy throne,
While worlds on worlds are Thine alone.

—MARTIN LUTHER, 1535

THE BOY JESUS

The Boy Jesus lingered behind.

—LUKE 2:43

IS YOUR HEART HEAVY FOR A LOVED ONE IN THE GRIP OF AN addiction or beset by problems? Are you a troubled parent, worried about your son or daughter?

The panic-stricken parents of Jesus knew the fear of losing a child, for a remarkable story is inscribed in Luke 2:41–50. Jesus, age twelve, accompanied His parents to Jerusalem for the Passover Feast. Imagine their alarm, while returning home, when they realized they had left Him behind. Joseph and Mary, thinking Him among friends and relatives, traveled a day's journey before it dawned on them He was missing.

Put yourself in their place. They had lost their own child! But more—they had lost God's only begotten Son who had been entrusted to their care. A day's journey, a second day's return, and three days' searching. It's every parent's nightmare: a twelve-year-old, missing five days in a daunting city. In whose bed did He sleep? How was He fed? We don't know.

Luke simply says,

After three days they found Him in the temple, sitting in the midst of the teachers, both listening to them and asking them questions. And all who heard Him were astonished at His understanding and answers. So when they saw Him, they were amazed; and His mother said to Him, "Son, why have You done this to us? Look, Your father and I have sought You anxiously." And He said to them, "Why did you seek Me? Did you not know that I must be about My Father's business?" (Luke 2:46–49)

The lessons: First, Jesus is never really AWOL; He has promised to never leave us or forsake us.

Second, He is always about His Father's business, which means He is continually working on our behalf and on behalf of our loved ones.

Third, it sometimes takes five days to resolve the problem, or five months or five years—or more. We may have extended burdens to bear, but when we listen to Christ we're astonished at His understanding and answers.

Fourth, Jesus is always amazed at our anxiety. Why should we doubt Him? Why should we fear? Even at age twelve, He had everything under control. So if you are anxious about that loved one today, seek out Jesus. He can claim their hearts and even more—He can calm your soul.

Come kneel before the radiant Boy
Who brings you beauty, peace, and joy.

—JEAN DE BREBEUF, C. 1643

$\mathcal{T}$HE SEED OF WOMAN

And I will put enmity
Between you and the woman,
And between your seed and her Seed;
He shall bruise your head,
And you shall bruise His heel.

—Genesis 3:15

God is shock-proof. You and I may reel from un-expected blows, but our Lord has already anticipated everything. He's never caught short. He can deal with whatever you're facing today. He has, after all, already dealt with the worst tragedy to occur in human history: the sin of Adam and Eve that plunged the world into the gloomy cave of endless suffering. God knew it would happen, and He prepared a solution before the world began.

Genesis 3:15 gives us the Bible's earliest promise of a coming Redeemer and Messiah, whom God referred to here as the Seed of Woman. Remarkably, God spoke these words to Satan and had them recorded for our benefit. In seducing Eve, the devil thought he had gained an ally in his rebellion against the Almighty. But the Lord turned the tables, telling Satan:

1. *I will put enmity between you and the woman.* In other words, instead of gaining an ally, the human race will loathe and abhor the satanic.

2. *I will put enmity between your children and Eve's great Child—the Messiah.* The Seed of Woman—the Redeemer—shall come as the great archenemy of all that is evil.

3. *He will destroy you.* Like a man crushing the head of a rattlesnake, the Seed of Woman will defeat and destroy the serpent.

4. *You will hurt Him.* In the process, the Messiah Himself will be bruised. His heel will be pierced.

Long centuries later, Jesus Christ writhed in pain as the spike entered His heel like a serpent's fang, affixing Him to the cross. But on that cross, Satan and all his works were trampled. The devil's head was crushed, just as predicted.

God knows the future as well as He knows the past, and the present is unfolding as He knew it would. He isn't surprised; He's prepared just now for whatever you're facing. The Seed of Woman, who has already won the final victory, is near at hand to help you in the battles along the way.

Rise, the woman's conqu'ring Seed,
Bruise in us the serpent's head.
Now display Thy saving power,
Ruined nature now restore.

—CHARLES WESLEY, 1739

THE DAYSPRING FROM ON HIGH

Through the tender mercy of our God,
With which the Dayspring from on high has visited us;
To give light to those who sit in darkness and the shadow of death,
To guide our feet into the way of peace.

—LUKE 1:78–79

WHAT'S A "DAYSPRING"?

When I consulted the dictionary, I found *daybed, daybreak, daydream,* and *daylight*—but no listing for *dayspring.* Turning to my Greek dictionaries, I found that Luke used the word *anatole.* It's found ten times in the New Testament and is usually translated "east." Literally, however, it has to do with the rising of the sun.

Jesus is our Sunrise!

In his classic book *Walden,* Henry David Thoreau wrote about the early hours of the morning: "I got up early and bathed in the pond; that was a religious exercise and one of the best things which I did. . . . The morning, which is the most memorable season of the day, is the awakening hour. . . . All memorable events, I should say, transpire in morning time and in a morning atmosphere. . . . To be awake is to be alive."[2]

The human race was caught in an endless night, a night without stars or moon, without hope or glittering of joy. Then Jesus came— the Bright and Morning Star, the Dayspring from on High, the rising orb of fire—massive and marvelous—illuminating the cosmos.

You and I were caught in an endless night of sin and shame, without hope or direction. Then Jesus came—and we who sat in darkness and in the shadow of death have seen a great light. As John said, "In Him was life, and the life was the light of men" (1:4).

Many people are caught in an emotional night of sadness and depression. But Jesus is our Dayspring. Every moment is morning for the Christian. Life is an endless day, and the warmth of His rays

His Nativity Names

keeps a glow on our faces whatever the circumstances. He's the incandescent bulb inside the heart. Today, shake off dread and darkness and wash your face in a bath of praise.

Son of Righteousness, arise,
Triumph o'er the shades of night;
Dayspring from on high be near;
Day-star, in my heart appear.

—CHARLES WESLEY, 1740

THE CONSOLATION OF ISRAEL

And behold, there was a man in Jerusalem whose name was Simeon, and this man was just and devout, waiting for the Consolation of Israel.

—LUKE 2:25

CONSOLATION?

To us, the term conveys second-best—as in consolation prize. "Sorry you didn't win the million dollars, but here's a box of chocolate."

But it's a better word than that. The root word—*console*—means "to soothe the grief of another, to comfort, to give solace." The Greek word is almost identical to the word "Comforter" found in John 14, when Jesus, referring to the Holy Spirit, told the disciples that He would give them "another Comforter" (v. 16 KJV).

I've received consolation many times in life: when my parents passed away, in the face of bitter disappointments, when trials have disheartened me. My most vivid recollection of consolation, however, involves the death of a dog. My little Tippy was my good-natured, mixed-breed best friend. We were inseparable. Just a tiny dog, he rode in my bicycle basket, and we spent years together flying down hills, swimming in rivers, falling asleep together, and waking up on the same pillow.

When he died, I was desolate. That evening, my dad pulled me onto his lap and talked to me about it. "Tippy was getting awfully old," he said. "His teeth were bad, and it was getting hard for him to eat. . . ." He told me it was better that Tippy had gone on to "dog heaven." I curled into his chest and cried, but his words softened the terrible sting of grief, making it bearable.

That's a pale example of what Jesus does for us. Sometimes not a soul on earth can console us. But He knows how to take us in His arms and soothe our hearts with His comfort. He is the God of All

Comfort. He uses His Word. He uses quiet moments. He uses solitude. He uses the trials of life. He uses the hymnbook. He's the Consolation of Israel, and He's our Consoler too.

If you are weary or worried today, lean heavily on Him and let His consoling care soften the sting of grief and make it bearable. Let Him impart His joy!

Come, Thou long expected Jesus, born to set Thy people free;
From our fears and sins release us, let us find our rest in Thee.
Israel's strength and consolation, Hope of all the earth Thou art;
Dear desire of every nation, Joy of every longing heart.

—CHARLES WESLEY, 1744

ᴛʜᴇ ʜᴏʀɴ ᴏғ sᴀʟᴠᴀᴛɪᴏɴ

Blessed is the Lord God of Israel,
For He has . . . raised up a horn of salvation for us
In the house of His servant David.

—Lᴜᴋᴇ 1:68–69

Tʜɪs ɪs ᴀ ᴛɪᴛʟᴇ ғᴏʀ Cʜʀɪsᴛ ᴛʜᴀᴛ ᴍᴇᴀɴs ᴀʟᴍᴏsᴛ ɴᴏᴛʜɪɴɢ to us today, for most of us didn't grow up on farms. The only cattle horns we see are decorations on the walls of steak houses and Western-themed restaurants. To people of Bible times, however, this picture instantly brought to their minds the idea of might and power, even of panic and terror.

Perhaps you can identify if you've ever been to a state fair. In the livestock arena are huge, prize-winning oxen or bulls. They weigh a ton, and their massive heads are punctuated with enormous horns ending in razor-like tips. Oxen and bulls don't smile, and the black gleam in their eyes can make you shudder. What if one of those massive animals got loose? What kind of damage could those horns inflict? We can see ourselves being disemboweled in about a second!

No wonder David cried in Psalm 22:21: "Save me from the mouth of the lions; / save me from the horns of the wild oxen" (NIV).

When the Bible writers wanted to visualize God's power on our behalf, this was the figure they used. Can you picture God as a mighty force using His sharpest weapons on your behalf? Jesus is the power and might of God, His not-so-secret weapon.

But wait! There's more. Animal horns also served as the first trumpets in human history. Musicians learned to blow them with great effect. Their battle cry could be heard by the entire army. "It shall come to pass, when they make a long blast with the ram's horn, and when you hear the sound of the trumpet, that all the people shall shout with a great shout; then the wall of the city will fall down flat" (Josh. 6:5).

So there's a double meaning: both power and proclamation. Good works on our behalf and good news for our souls. That's our Jesus—the Horn of our Salvation.

O tell me the story that never grows old,
The story of One Whom the prophets foretold;
The Horn of salvation, the Scepter and Star,
The Light in the darkness they saw from afar.

—JAMES M. GRAY, 1901

HER FIRSTBORN SON

She . . . brought forth her firstborn Son.
And [Joseph] called His name JESUS.

—MATTHEW 1:25

WHEN THE GREAT EVANGELIST D. L. MOODY DIED, ONE OF his associates wrote a little booklet entitled, *Why God Used D. L. Moody*. Borrowing that idea, I'd like to tell you why the Lord used the lowly virgin Mary. What was so special about this teenager? Of all the women of Jewish antiquity, why was she alone chosen to bear and raise the Messiah?

First, she was sold out to God. When the angel commissioned her as the Messiah's mother, her humble response was: "I am the Lord's servant. May it be to me as you have said" (Luke 1:38 NIV). In other words, "Whatever, whenever, wherever You say, Lord. I'm perpetually at Your disposal." Have you made that kind of carte blanche commitment to Christ?

Second, she was a woman of faith. In describing Mary, the Bible gives us one of the best definitions of faith to be found between the covers of Scripture: "Blessed is she who has believed that what the Lord has said to her will be accomplished!" (Luke 1:45 NIV). Are you troubled and worried today? Have faith! Faith is simply believing that what the Lord has said will be accomplished.

Third, she was a woman with a personal commitment to sexual purity. The most frequently used word describing her is "virgin." She understood that true love waits until marriage, a practice that was perhaps as rare in biblical times as it is today.

Fourth, Mary knew how to praise the Lord. "My soul glorifies the Lord," she sang in Luke 1:46-47, "and my spirit rejoices in God my Savior" (NIV).

Finally, Mary was a woman who filled herself with Scripture. In reading the hymn she composed in Luke 1:46–55, I'm amazed at how she wove together so many Old Testament verses, Scriptures, and themes. They flowed from her like springs from a reservoir.

Do you want to be someone God uses in great ways? His eyes are ranging throughout the earth, looking for someone committed to personal purity, who is sold out to Him, full of faith, full of praise, and full of His Word.

That can be you!

A great and mighty wonder, a full and holy cure:
The virgin bears the Infant with virgin honor pure!
Repeat the hymn again: "To God on high be glory
And peace on earth to men!"

—SAINT GERMANUS, AD 734

 KING

Pilate therefore said to Him, "Are You a king then?"
Jesus answered, "You say rightly that I am a king.
For this cause I was born, and for this cause I have come into the
world, that I should bear witness to the truth. Everyone who is of the
truth hears My voice."

—JOHN 18:37

WE HAVE TWO KINDS OF KINGS IN THIS WORLD. THE FIRST IS the parliamentary monarch, such as Britain's Queen Elizabeth II. As the object of great reverence, she is encircled by grandeur and gilded with tradition. In terms of real power, however, she has little; her opinions are heard with politeness and patience, but her office is primarily ceremonial. The British prime minister holds the reins of government.

The other kind of king is the absolute monarch whose office is both ceremonially impressive and politically powerful. He is head of state, he leads the nation, and his authority is supreme.

Many Christians treat Jesus like a parliamentary king. Once a week—if it's convenient!—they hold court with Him and make Him the object of great reverence. He is heard with politeness and patience, but in terms of daily life He has little influence.

Our Lord is an absolute monarch. He would rather have one person who is 100 percent committed to him than a hundred people who are 80 percent committed. John Wesley said, "If I had three hundred men who feared nothing but God, hated nothing but sin, and determined to know nothing among men but Christ, and Him crucified, I would set the world on fire."

"For the eyes of the LORD run to and fro throughout the whole earth, to show Himself strong on behalf of those whose heart is loyal to Him" (2 Chron. 16:9).

Queen Victoria once asked General William Booth, founder of the

Salvation Army, for the secret of his success. "I guess," replied Booth, "the reason is because God has all there is of me."

Does He have all there is of you?

—⊗—

Ye armies of the living God,
With banner, shield and sword,
March onward, shouting as you go,
"No king but Christ our Lord."

All crowns be on His sacred head,
All worlds be at His feet,
All scepters in His mighty hand,
All tongues His praise repeat.

—FANNY CROSBY, 1891

$\mathcal{A}$NOTHER KING

These are all acting contrary to the decrees of Caesar,
saying there is another king—Jesus.

—ACTS 17:7

SOME TIME AGO IN ENGLAND, I PURCHASED A BIOGRAPHY OF King George III by Christopher Hibbert. George III often escaped the confines of London by journeying to his home at Windsor Castle. While there, he took off by himself on long walks, and occasionally he surprised the neighbors by popping into their homes. One day King George walked into a barn where a woman was milking a cow. She had no idea that he was king.

George asked her where all the other laborers and farm workers had gone. They had all gone to see the king, the woman said, adding, "I wouldn't give a pin to see him. Besides the fools will lose a day's work by it, and that is more than I can afford to do. I have five children to work for." Taking some coins from his pocket, King George gave them to her. "Well, then," he said, "you may tell your companions who were gone to see the King that the King came to see you."[3]

That's just what God did when Jesus was born in Bethlehem. The King of kings and Lord of lords came to see us. He came to meet our needs. He wants to give us His life, His hope, His companionship.

While we go about our everyday labors, He is there. In our distress and despair, He is there. In our joys and sorrows, He is there.

He is the polyonymous Jesus, and His many names reflect His gifts to us. He is Christ. He is the Faithful Witness, the Firstborn from the Dead, the Ruler over the Kings of the Earth. He is Him Who Loved Us, who washed us with His own blood, and who has made us to be a kingdom of priests and kings. God has given Him a name that is above every name, that at the name of Jesus every knee should bow, and every tongue confess that He is Lord, to the glory of God the Father.

Behold, another King! Behold your King.

> *The King of kings lay thus in lowly manger,*
> *In all our trials born to be our Friend!*
> *He knows our need — to our weakness is no stranger.*
> *Behold your King; before Him lowly bend!*
> *Behold your King; before Him lowly bend!*

—PLACIDE CLAPPEAU, 1847

KING OF THE JEWS

Where is He who has been born King of the Jews?
THIS IS JESUS THE KING OF THE JEWS.

—MATTHEW 2:2, 27:37

THIS TITLE CIRCUMNAVIGATES THE EARTHLY LIFE OF CHRIST. At His birth the Magi sought Him who had been born King of the Jews. At His death, a sign affixed to His cross said, "THIS IS JESUS THE KING OF THE JEWS." This title was used of Christ eighteen times in the four Gospels—but only at the beginning and end of His life.

The word *king* is connected in its archaic background to the word *kin*. A king was someone of one's own group who was given a place of leadership. In Jewish history, the greatest dynasty was that of the humble shepherd, David, the youngest son of Jesse. From the loins of David, a great and coming king was promised to the Jewish people—one who would be both their kin and their king, one who would rule over the house of Israel forever.

And so He came.

He was born King of the Jews, and that's the way He died. Yet the nation of Israel as a whole didn't recognize His royalty or submit to His rule.

But they will. The entire Bible anticipates a day when He shall sit on the throne of Israel and reign over Jerusalem, over Israel, and over all the earth: "Of the increase of His government and peace / There shall be no end, / Upon the throne of David and over His kingdom" (Isa. 9:7).

This was the favorite theme of the devotional writer, Frances Ridley Havergal. In her little book *Your King,* published in 1876, she wrote: "He knows the hopeless anarchy of a heart without a king. Is there a more desolate cry than 'We have no king'?—none to reverence and love, none to obey, none to guide and protect and rule over us, none to keep us in the truest freedom of whole-hearted loyalty.

How glad we are that He Himself is our King. For we are so sure that He is able even to subdue all things unto Himself in this inner kingdom which we cannot govern at all."[4]

What an interesting phrase, "this inner kingdom which we cannot govern." I have one of those. My habits. My thoughts. My attitudes. My appetites. My desires. Without Christ, they're out of control, ungovernable, unmanageable. Only He who created me is wise and strong enough to take the reins of my interior life. I've found, as perhaps you have, that I'm happiest when my heart-throne is occupied by the King of the Jews!

Reign over me, Lord Jesus!
Oh, make my heart Thy throne!
It shall be Thine forever,
It shall be Thine alone!

—FRANCES RIDLEY HAVERGAL, 1876

KING OF KINGS

And He has on His robe and on His thigh a name written:
KING OF KINGS.

—REVELATION 19:16

MANY YEARS AGO, I READ A BIOGRAPHY OF ENGLAND'S KING Edward VII, son of good Queen Victoria. Because of his mother's longevity, Edward didn't become king until he was an old man, and he spent most of his life creating one scandal after another. He indulged freely in women, food, drink, gambling, sports, and travel. His extramarital activities continued well into his sixties, and he was implicated in several divorce cases. He rose to the throne upon his mother's death in 1901 and died nine years later.

But there's more to the story. One day, a great prayer warrior named Edwin Joseph Evans was vacationing in America. In the Adirondacks, he set aside time for prayer and the study of the Word. One morning, Evans arose with a great burden to pray for King Edward's conversion. A sense of urgency grew throughout the day, and Evans devoted himself to earnest prayer. The following morning came word from a Welsh companion: "King Edward is dead!"[5]

Years passed, and Dr. Evans was dining with another British church leader, Dr. J. Gregory Mantle. During the dinner, Dr. Mantle said, "Did you know that Edward VII was saved on his deathbed?"

Pressed for details, Mantle said:

> *The king was in France when he was taken ill. He was brought to England and there was hope that he might recover. However, there came a turn for the worse. At that time, His Majesty called one of his lords-in-waiting and ordered him to go to Paternoster Row and secure for him a copy of a tract which his mother, Queen Victoria, had given to him when he was a lad. It was entitled* The Sinner's Friend. *After much searching, the lord-in-waiting found the tract, brought it*

to His Majesty, and upon reading it, King Edward VII made earnest repentance and received the Lord Jesus as his Savior.

Scanning the world for a dedicated prayer warrior, God directed a heavy heart-burden on Joe Evans in the Adirondacks, resulting in the King of England's meeting the King of kings in the nick of time. When we talk with the King of kings, even the rulers of earth are susceptible to the influence of our prayers.

How rich Thy bounty, King of kings!
Thy favors, how divine!
The blessings which Thy Gospel brings,
How splendidly they shine!

—PHILIP DODDRIDGE, 1739

KING OF RIGHTEOUSNESS

Melchizedek . . . first being translated "king of righteousness."

—HEBREWS 7:1–2

THE OLD TESTAMENT CHARACTER MELCHIZEDEK WAS A proto-type of Christ, and the very word *Melchizedek* comes from smaller words that combine to form the meaning "king of righteousness." It's one of our Lord's royal titles.

The Bible often uses the words *holy* and *righteous* to describe God. Holiness refers to the essence of God's being. He is utterly pure, and the concentration of His purity outshines a billion suns.

God's righteousness is the application of that purity in His actions. Because He is holy within Himself, He is righteous toward us. One theologian expressed it like this: "God is, in His essence, by His very nature, holiness itself; and righteousness is the mode or way by which His essence is expressed toward His created world or toward anything apart from Himself."[6]

I have a King who will never embarrass or disappoint me. No scandal can ever diminish His legacy. No moral failure will tarnish His reign. He cannot sin nor fail to keep His word. His promises will never go unfulfilled. He is holy in all His ways and righteous in all His deeds.

But even better: He wants to impute His righteousness to me, so that in His sight I am just as righteous as the King of Righteousness. I can never on my own merits stand in the King's presence. I'm a broken sinner. I've created my own little scandals. Moral failure has tarnished my life. I cannot help breaking my promises. But the King transferred my sins to His account while, at the same time, transferring His righteousness to my account.

This righteousness from God comes through faith in Jesus Christ to all who believe. There is no difference, for all have sinned and fall short of the glory of God, and are justified freely by his grace through the redemption that came by Christ Jesus. God presented him as a sacrifice of atonement, through faith in his blood. (Romans 3:22–25 NIV)

Why did Jesus do this for us?

Drop the last letter from *king* and you have the answer. We are made in His image. We are His kin: "Therefore, in all things He had to be made like His brethren, that He might be a merciful and faithful High Priest in things pertaining to God, to make propitiation for the sins of the people" (Heb. 2:17). Think of Him as your righteousness.

Come, and begin Thy reign
Of everlasting peace;
Come, take the kingdom to Thyself,
Great King of Righteousness.

—HORATIUS BONAR, 1846

THE PRINCE

Know therefore and understand,
That from the going forth of the command
To restore and build Jerusalem
Until Messiah the Prince,
There shall be seven weeks and sixty-two weeks;
The street shall be built again, and the wall,
Even in troublesome times.
And after the sixty-two weeks Messiah shall be cut off,
but not for Himself.

—DANIEL 9:25–26

JESUS IS BOTH KING AND PRINCE, SINCE HE IS BOTH GOD THE Son and the Son of God. The word *prince* is made up of the prefix *primus,* meaning "first," and the stem word *capere,* meaning "to take." He takes first place.

In using this title for the Messiah in Daniel 9, the Old Testament actually pinpoints the exact time of His first coming. This passage requires some digging, but its calculations, which are remarkably precise, form an important piece of evidence for the authenticity of our Lord's messianic identity. It also gives us an incredible calendar for the future.

In response to his earnest prayers, Daniel was told that God's program for the human race would be consummated in seventy "sevens" (v. 24 NIV). Since "sevens" here refers to years, this would be 490 years (70 x 7 = 490).

The first sixty-nine "sevens"—or 483 years—began with the decree to restore and rebuild Jerusalem. There were four such decrees, but the one referred to here appears to be the fourth and last decree, issued by the Persian King Artaxerxes on March 5, 444 BC, as recorded in Nehemiah 2.

From that decree, there were seven "sevens" (49 years), followed by sixty-two "sevens" (434 years). That makes a total of 483 years between the issuing of the decree in 444 BC and the time when Messiah the Prince would be "cut off."

The Jewish calendar was made up of 360 days per year. When converted to our Gregorian calendar, the end of these 483 years fell exactly at the time of our Lord's triumphal entry into Jerusalem when He presented Himself as Israel's Messiah Prince.[7]

He came and was "cut off, but not for Himself"—it was for you and me.

Hidden away in the mysterious prophecies of the Old Testament is a remarkable prediction—later fulfilled in exacting detail—giving us the very date of our Lord's triumphal entry. No wonder faith comes by hearing, and hearing by the Word of God. The more we study the Scripture, the more it convinces us of its own authority.

All hail to the Prince of Life!
Hosanna to Him we sing—
He comes as a mighty Victor,
He comes as a conq'ring King!

—MRS. R. N. THOMAS, 1900

THE PRINCE OF PEACE

And His name will be called . . . Prince of Peace.
—Isaiah 9:6

NORMA PATTERSON OF PORTLAND, OREGON, CALLED ME THE other day and told me about her aged parents. When they were in their nineties—her father was 93—she came by to take them shopping. Her dad was in apparent good health for his age and had recently bought a tiller to use in his garden. The couple had their devotions together each morning, and on this particular morning, the old gentleman had focused on a verse that said: "Peace I leave with you; my peace I give you. I do not give to you as the world gives. Do not let your hearts be troubled and do not be afraid" (John 14:28 NIV). They shared that with Norma, then the old fellow went over to the easy chair to sit and wait for the shopping trip. He dozed off. When they tried to awaken him a few minutes later, he was in heaven.

"How thankful we were," Norma told me, "for that final Scripture verse that served as the closing benediction to my father's earthly life."

When Jesus spoke those words in John 14:27, He was speaking as the Prince of Peace, but His disciples were subjects of fear. For them, it was a night of sheer terror. Later that very evening, Jesus was seized, bound, and led away to be whipped and slain. The disciples fled like meteors lost in space. Only gradually did they understand the plan of God, the power of His promises, the reality of His resurrection, and the depths of His protective companionship.

I don't know about you, but I must sometimes sit myself down and give myself a little sermon about the Prince of Peace. I'm a jittery soul that has to consciously appropriate God's promised peace. One of the things that helps me most is searching out and memorizing some of the wonderful verses in the book of Isaiah about God's peace, such as: "His name shall be called . . . the Prince of Peace. Of the increase of

His government and peace there will be no end . . . But He was wounded for our transgressions, He was bruised for our iniquities; the chastisement of our peace was upon Him . . . You shall go out with joy, and be led out with peace . . . Lord, You will establish peace for us . . . You will keep him in perfect peace, whose mind is stayed on You, because He trusts in You" (Isaiah 9:6-7; 53:5; 55:12; 26:12; 26:3).

Someone once said, "Our day tends to go the way the corners of our mouths are turned." Today fix your mind on the Prince of Peace. Go out with joy and be led out with peace.

⬥

His Name shall be the Prince of Peace,
Forevermore adorned,
The Wonderful, the Counselor,
The great and mighty Lord.

—JOHN MORISON, 1781

RINCE AND SAVIOR

Him God has exalted to His right hand to be Prince and Savior, to give repentance to Israel and forgiveness of sins. And we are His witnesses.

—Acts 5:31–32

THOSE WORDS COST PETER A BEATING. HE AND HIS COL-leagues were on trial before the Sanhedrin, the national counsel of ancient Israel. The text says:

> *When they had brought them, they set them before the council. And the high priest asked them, saying, "Did we not strictly command you not to teach in this name? And look, you have filled Jerusalem with your doctrine, and intend to bring this Man's blood on us!" But Peter and the other apostles answered and said: "We ought to obey God rather than men. The God of our fathers raised up Jesus whom you murdered by hanging him on a tree. Him God has exalted to His right hand to be Prince and Savior." (5:27–31)*

After some discussion, the Sanhedrin decided to flog the apostles, a typical but painful form of Jewish punishment consisting of thirty-nine welts laid across the back by a strong arm bearing a flexible rod.

> *And when they had called for the apostles and beaten them, they commanded that they should not speak in the name of Jesus, and let them go. So they departed from the presence of the council, rejoicing that they were counted worthy to suffer shame for His name. And daily in the temple, and in every house, they did not cease teaching and preaching Jesus as the Christ. (5:40–42)*

This is the same Peter, of course, who only weeks before had cowered in the presence of the servant girl of the high priest. But now he had seen the risen Christ. Now he'd been filled with the Holy Spirit. Now he had an irrepressible message and an unstoppable mission.

People are still being whipped for their faith. As you read these words, multitudes of believers are behind bars, chained, threatened, and facing death. I'm looking just now at the newspaper headlines on my desk: "Pastor Shot Dead in Pulpit." A Presbyterian pastor in Indonesia was killed while preaching in Central Sulawei, Indonesia.

None of us know when we'll be called on to suffer for our faith. But we have a risen Christ, a Prince, a Savior. We're out to change the world for Him, and we must obey God rather than men.

Bring near Thy great salvation, Thou Lamb for sinners slain;
Fill up the roll of Thine elect, then take Thy power, and reign;
Appear, Desire of nations, Thine exiles long for home;
Show in the heaven Thy promised sign; Thou Prince and Savior, come.

—HENRY ALFORD, 1867

LORD

The voice of one crying in the wilderness:
"Prepare the way of the LORD."

—MATTHEW 3:3

THE WORD *Lord* OCCURS 696 TIMES IN THE NEW TESTA-
ment, almost always referring to Christ Jesus. As the New Testament
authors wrote it in the original Greek, the word was *kurios*, which
had a range of meanings in the ancient culture, from the common
"sir" to "landowner" to "sovereign."

When Jerome translated this word into Latin, the word became
dominus. From that come several well-known English words, including *dominant* and *dominoes*.

Dominoes?

The Dominicus monks reportedly loved this game in earlier centuries. Wearing their domino-like black and white hoods, they called
out the Latin word *Dominium*, meaning "Dominate," whenever one
had used his last tile and won the game. Another version of the story
says that the monks played this game during periods of silence when
they could only say the words, *"Benedicamus domino* [Let us bless the
Lord]."

The lordship of Christ, however, is no game. In Matthew 7:21,
Jesus warned, "Not everyone who says to Me, 'Lord, Lord,' shall
enter the kingdom of heaven, but he who does the will of My Father
in heaven."

There's no gentle way to put it. The nature of lordship is domina-
tion, and Christ wants to dominate our lives, to dominate our thinking, to dominate our affections, to dominate our schedules, to
dominate our attitudes. Not in aggressive hostility, but in loving wisdom. He wants us to say, in the words of Adelaide Pollard's hymn:
"Have Thine own way, Lord! Have Thine own way! Thou art the
Potter, I am the clay."

There came a day when I was a college sophomore that I knelt and turned my life over to Christ, as fully and completely as I knew how. I've never been the same since that moment, and I've never regretted it for a second.

Missionary C. T. Studd put it this way: "If Jesus Christ be God and died for me, then no sacrifice can be too great for me to make for Him."

Is He the Lord of all there is of your life?

Who is on the Lord's side? Who will serve the King?
Who will be His helpers, other lives to bring?
Who will leave the world's side? Who will face the foe?
Who is on the Lord's side? Who for Him will go?
By Thy call of mercy, by Thy grace divine,
We are on the Lord's side—Savior, we are Thine!

—FRANCES HAVERGAL, 1877

LORD OF THE SABBATH

Therefore the Son of Man is also Lord of the Sabbath.

—MARK 2:28

LESLIE FLYNN, PASTOR EMERITUS OF GRACE BAPTIST Church in Nanuet, New York, and the writer of over forty highly readable books, tells of seven unmarried brothers who lived together in a large house. Six went out to work each day, but one stayed home. He had the place warm and all lit up when the other six arrived home from their places of labor. He also had a delicious, full-course dinner on the table for his hungry brothers.

One day the six brothers decided that the one that had been staying home should go to work. "It's not fair," they said, "for one to stay home while the others slave at a job." So they made the seventh brother find work too. But when they all came home the first night, there was no light, nor was there any warmth; and worst of all, there was no hearty dinner awaiting them. And the next night the same thing: darkness, cold, hunger. They soon went back to their former arrangement.

It is the day of rest and worship that keeps the other six bright, warm, and nourishing. "When we desecrate the Lord's Day," said Flynn, "we only hurt ourselves."[8]

If God wanted to rest on the seventh day, how much more necessary is it for us!

Jesus is the Lord of Monday through Saturday, too, of course, but in a special way He wants to dominate and regulate our Sundays. It's to be a day focused on Him, on His wonderful Word, on His blessed presence, and on the reality of His glorious resurrection that He accomplished on the first day of the week. But for most of us, Sunday has gone from a holy day to a holiday to a hollow day. It's become a day for shopping, banking, traveling, and sports. Someone observed that our grandparents called it the Holy Sabbath. Our parents called it the Lord's Day. We call it Sunday. And our children call it the weekend. See how we have denigrated this special day? From Holy Sabbath to a mere weekend.

Is He still Lord of the Sabbath? Lord of your Sabbath?

Lord of the Sabbath, hear us pray,
In this Your house, on this Your day;
And own, as grateful sacrifice,
The songs which from Your temple rise.

Now met to pray and bless Your Name,
Whose mercies flow each day the same;
Whose kind compassions never cease,
We seek instruction, pardon, peace.

—PHILIP DODDRIDGE, 1737

LORD OF ALL

The word which God sent to the children of Israel, preaching peace through Jesus Christ — He is Lord of all — that word you know, which was proclaimed throughout all Judea, and began from Galilee after the baptism which John preached.

—Acts 10:36–37

THIS IS THE ONLY TIME IN THE NEW TESTAMENT THAT ANY-one called Jesus "Lord of all." Three Old Testament references describe God as "Lord of all the earth" (Josh. 3:11, 13; Zech. 6:5). The implication seems to be His total supremacy. There is nothing over which He is not absolute ruler and final authority. In personal terms, it causes each of us to ask ourselves, *Is Jesus Christ Lord of all there is in my life?*

In my files is a clipping about a Haitian pastor illustrating to his congregation the need for total commitment to Christ. He told of a certain man who wanted to sell his house for two thousand dollars. Another family badly wanted it but couldn't afford the full price. After much haggling, the owner agreed to sell the house for half the asking price with just one stipulation: he would retain ownership of one small nail protruding from just over the door.

After several years, the original owner wanted the house back, but the new owners were unwilling to sell. So the first owner went out, found the carcass of a dead dog, and hung it from the single nail he still owned. Soon the house became uninhabitable, and the family was forced to sell the house to the owner of the nail.

The Haitian pastor's conclusion: "If we leave the devil with even one small peg in our life, he will return to hang his rotting garbage on it, making it unfit for Christ's habitation."

In other words, if Jesus isn't Lord of all, He isn't Lord at all. Are we ready to say, as Jesus Himself did, "Not My will, but Thine be done"?

There comes a time in our Christian lives when we realize that the essence of Christianity isn't soft pews but hard choices. It isn't enough to have Christ included in our thinking; He must be at the spinning core of our hearts and minds. Not everyone who says to Him, "Lord, Lord!" will enter the kingdom of heaven, but those who really acknowledge Him as Lord of life, practicing His lordship so as to "[do] the will of My Father in heaven" (Matt. 7:21).

Wherever He is, He must rule. He must be Lord of all, or not at all.

All hail the power of Jesus' Name!
Let angels prostrate fall.
Bring forth the royal diadem
And crown Him Lord of all.

—EDWARD PERRONET, 1779

MY LORD AND MY GOD

And Thomas answered and said to Him, "My Lord and My God!"

—JOHN 20:28

THOMAS WAS THE GREATEST SKEPTIC AMONG THE DISCIPLES. He was so wary of the Resurrection rumors he didn't even show up on Easter evening, and so cynical he didn't believe the eyewitness accounts later. "Unless I see in His hands the print of the nails, and put my finger into the print of the nails, and put my hand into His side, I will not believe," he said (John 20:25).

But exactly one week later, Thomas came face-to-face with the risen Christ, and he exclaimed, "My Lord and my God!"

What then happened to Thomas? The book of Acts gives little information about him. Luke, the author of Acts, focused on the ministries of Peter and Paul, telling us the story of the gospel's march from Jerusalem to Rome, the center of the empire. But from other sources, we know more about Thomas's life than of virtually any of the other disciples' lives.

While Peter and Paul were taking the gospel westward into Europe, Thomas was traveling eastward with the same news. He was apostle to the vast lands of India. William Steuart McBirnie, in his fascinating book *The Search for the Twelve Apostles,* wrote, "No one can estimate how many millions of Christians came to believe in Christ because of St. Thomas. They are beyond counting. The churches which St. Thomas founded in India have kept Christianity alive and extended the faith which survives to this day."[9]

According to our best sources, Thomas's ministry came to an end when he died a martyr's death—he was pierced through with a lance—on a mountain (now called Mount Thomas) outside the city of Madras. His tomb may be visited to this day.

What could have been so powerful, so convincing, as to transform a depressed skeptic into a worldwide evangelist whose energy never flagged, whose faith never faltered, and whose gospel never changed?

Thomas saw Jesus, risen and alive. He heard the Lord Jesus say, "Reach your finger here, and look at My hands; and reach your hand here, and put it into My side. Do not be unbelieving, but believing" (John 20:27).

And from that moment, Thomas belonged to his Lord and his God.

Jesus, my Lord, my God, my All,
Hear me, blest Savior, when I call;
Hear me, and from Thy dwelling place
Pour down the riches of Thy grace;
Jesus, my Lord, I Thee adore;
O make me love Thee more and more.

—HENRY A. COLLINS, 1854

LORD OF THE DEAD AND THE LIVING

For to this end Christ died and rose and lived again,
that He might be Lord of both the dead and the living.

—ROMANS 14:9

LORD OF THE DEAD? WHAT A STRANGE TITLE FOR CHRIST, but how wonderful! Lord of the Living too! While we're alive on earth, Jesus is our Lord. When we die in Christ, He is still our Lord. Our hearts may miss a beat, but the lordship of Christ doesn't. Jesus made the case for the immortality of the soul when He pointed out the present-tense nature of the verb "am" in God's statement, "I am the God of Abraham, Isaac, and Jacob" (see Matt. 22:32). He was their God, and He still is, for they are still living, only in heaven.

This truth was of enormous comfort to me when my own parents, both committed Christians, passed away. I was close to both my dad and mom, and as a child I worried that something might happen to them. Fortunately I was middle-aged before they died, and the Lord gave me specific verses to sustain me in sorrow.

Though my father had been in frail health for some time, he was still trying to care for his invalid brother, who was comatose at a veterans' hospital. My dad apparently blacked out while returning home one day, wrecking his truck. Night after night, we stayed at the hospital as he hovered between life and death in the intensive-care ward. One evening as I tossed in bed, a verse of Scripture came to mind so forcibly that I've never forgotten it: "For I consider that the sufferings of this present time are not worthy to be compared with the glory which shall be revealed" (Rom. 8:18).

Years later, news came of my mother's death. It was early morning, and I staggered to the shower in a state of numbness, trying to dress and catch a flight home. Out of nowhere, a verse flashed to mind that gave me a peace that has never left: "Precious in the sight of the LORD / Is the death of His saints" (Ps. 116:15).

I praise God for the reassuring truths of those two verses. Jesus is our Lord whether we're alive on earth or alive in heaven. He is Lord of the Dead and the Living. "To live is Christ, and to die is gain" (Phil. 1:21).

$$\text{---}\mathcal{S}\text{---}$$

And let this feeble body fail,
And let it droop and die;
My soul shall quit the mournful vale,
And soar to worlds on high.

—CHARLES WESLEY, 1759

THE RIGHTEOUS JUDGE

There is in store for me the crown of righteousness,
which the Lord, the righteous Judge, will award to me on that day—
and not only to me, but also to all who have longed for his appearing.

—2 TIMOTHY 4:8 (NIV)

ONE MORNING SEVERAL MONTHS AGO, I ROSE IN THE WEE hours and drove to Fort Campbell, Kentucky, where hundreds of people had gathered in the predawn chill to await a battalion of soldiers returning from Iraq. My close friend, Steven Pierce, was among them, and I wanted to be there to welcome him and his men home.

Steven had shipped out immediately after seeing his little boy born, and now Madden was a toddler. Others of the soldiers had never seen their children, some of whom were almost a year old. Many mothers were there, holding babies, awaiting their husbands. The troops had been away longer than expected, almost a full year.

Children, parents, grandparents, girlfriends and boyfriends, brothers and sisters—hundreds of us shivered in the cold, but without complaint. Emotions ran high because Steven's platoon had been ambushed, and the ensuing intense firefight had taken the life of one of our men, Specialist Brandon Rowe. Steven himself had been wounded in battle, and it was near-miraculous that any of the men had survived.

Now they were almost home. Over the loudspeakers came the announcement that the planes were approaching. With hundreds of others, I filed from the hangar onto the tarmac and strained to see into the darkness. A few minutes later, a shout went up, then a roar of delight. Two tiny specks, taillights blinking in the distance, approached as though in slow motion. Finally the planes rolled up to the hangar, and as the soldiers disembarked, there were shouts, cries, tears, and the popping of flashbulbs. The troops lined up in formation, and shortly afterward the words came: "Fall out!"

Instantly the hangar became a sea of hugs, embraces, touches, and tears. If the combined emotion in that building could have been harnessed, I think it would have powered every factory in America. I've never experienced so much emotion in such a concentrated time and place, and I'll never forget it.

Only later did this thought come to me: *Are we equally emotional, equally eager for our Lord's return?* Are we awaiting the announcing blast of the trumpet? Casting a yearning eye to the sky? Waiting for that moment when the Lord's army will "fall out" and be "caught up"? Am I aching for that crown of righteousness which the Lord, the Righteous Judge, will award to me on that day, and to all who love His appearing?

The Apostle Paul used this title to describe the One whose Second Coming he longed for. When He does come again, Jesus will come as a righteous dispenser of justice to the world. Those of us who are His blood-bought children will have no fear, for our judgment was dispensed at Calvary. For us, it is a crown.

I love His appearing, I do, (don't you?)
The glad day is nearing, 'tis true;
He will take us on high
Where the saints cannot die;
I love His appearing, don't you?

— THORO HARRIS, 1916

JUDGE OF THE LIVING AND THE DEAD

And He commanded us to preach to the people, and to testify that it is He who was ordained by God to be Judge of the living and the dead.

—Acts 10:42

WHEN I WAS GROWING UP IN THE MOUNTAINS, SOME OF the ministers on the Tennessee/North Carolina border were known as "hellfire-and-brimstone preachers" because every time they stood in the pulpit, their sermons scorched their listeners. They preached hard and long against sin—and to them most everything was a sin. I remember how offended my grandmother was when the visiting evangelist thundered away at her particular hairstyle, which was in vogue at the time.

Things have now gone to the opposite extreme. Sermons are so market-driven and positive that one seldom hears any hellfire and brimstone. Ministers say virtually nothing about judgment and condemnation. Few worship songs refer to the destructive power of sin. We're in danger of developing a hell-less Christianity and a gospel that demands no accountability.

But Jesus Christ is still the Judge of the Living and the Dead. In other words, He is the ultimate Judge over time and eternity, both now and forever. On four different occasions, the New Testament uses similar terminology to speak of our Lord Jesus in this matter:

- *He . . . was ordained by God to be Judge of the living and the dead. (Acts 10:42)*

- *To this end Christ died and rose and lived again, that He might be Lord of both the dead and the living. . . . So then each of us shall give account of himself to God. (Romans 14:9, 12)*

- *The Lord Jesus Christ . . . will judge the living and the dead at His appearing. (2 Timothy 4:1)*

⌒◡ They will give an account to Him who is ready to judge the living and the dead. (1 Peter 4:5)

It's time we see our Lord Jesus not only as the gentle Friend of sinners but as the one to whom the whole world must give account. Perhaps our lives would reflect more holiness and our pulpits ring with more power if we were a little less fashionable and a little more biblical in our presentation of the person and work of Jesus Christ.

Thou Judge of quick and dead, before Whose bar severe,
With holy joy, or guilty dread, we all shall soon appear;
Our cautioned souls prepare for that tremendous day,
And fill us now with watchful care, and stir us up to pray.

—CHARLES WESLEY, 1749

ONE HAVING AUTHORITY

And so it was, when Jesus had ended these sayings, that the people were astonished at His teaching, for He taught them as one having authority, and not as the scribes.

—MATTHEW 7:28–29

THESE VERSES DESCRIBE THE CROWD'S RESPONSE TO OUR Lord's Sermon on the Mount, the inaugural address of Christ's ministry. At age thirty, Jesus had left the confines of the carpenter's shop, laid aside His hammer and nails, walked to the lakeside, and uttered His first public sermon—the greatest address on practical ethics the world had ever heard.

He spoke with authority.

The phrase "But I say to you" occurs five times in the Sermon on the Mount, and ten times in the whole of Matthew's Gospel: "You have heard that it was said to those of old. . . . But I say to you . . ." (5:27–28); "I tell you . . ." (5:39); "Whoever hears these sayings of Mine, and does them, I will liken him to a wise man. . . . But everyone who hears these sayings of Mine, and does not do them, will be like a foolish man" (7:24, 26).

Other passages in the Gospels confirm our Lord's confidence in the supreme authority of His own words:

—☙ *Whoever is ashamed of Me and My words, of him the Son of Man will be ashamed when He comes in His own glory. (Luke 9:26)*

—☙ *He who hears My word and believes on Him who sent Me has everlasting life. (John 5:24)*

—☙ *If you abide in My word, you are My disciples indeed. (John 8:31)*

—☙ *If anyone keeps My word he shall never see death (John 8:51)*

—☙ *Heaven and earth will pass away, but My words will by no means pass away. (Matthew 24:35)*

The scribes taught as I do. They read the Scriptures, tried to interpret them rightly, and sought to apply the truths to their listeners. But when Jesus opened His mouth, it was clear that He didn't consider Himself a mere commentator. He was speaking as the very Author of Scripture.

He spoke with the voice of Author-ity. His sermons were all in first person. All authority has been given to Him, and that authority is conveyed through His Word. The whole of Scripture is inspired and infallible, but there's something about those red letters that rings with the unconquerable. So read with confidence the Word of the Lord, knowing He rules over your life in all things!

His kingly word shall be with pow'r,
When Jesus speaks to me;
Grace for the needs of ev'ry hour,
When Jesus speaks to me.

—ELIZA HEWITT, 1915

GOVERNOR

*And thou Bethlehem, in the land of Judah, art not the least
among the princes of Juda: for out of thee shall come
a Governor, that shall rule my people Israel.*

—MATTHEW 2:6 (KJV)

THIS QUAINT RENDERING USES THE WORD *Governor* TO DE-
scribe the Babe of Bethlehem. The word *governor*, of course, is related
to the word *government,* and it conveys the idea of rule and authority.

Jesus, the head of the governments of heaven and earth, seeks to be
the Governor of your life and mine.

Millions of people go to church each week having a passing ac-
quaintance with Jesus of Nazareth, even calling Him "Lord." But He
isn't at the center of their lives or enthroned in their hearts. He
doesn't dominate their thinking, control their attitudes, or empower
their service. He isn't given His rightful place as Governor.

In 1904, the famous Bible teacher F. B. Meyer, speaking at the
Keswick Conference in England, gave this personal testimony:

> *I remember so well when He came to my heart and challenged me as
> to the keys of the fortress [of my life]. I had them upon my bunch, and
> before I gave them to Him I put one small key in my pocket. Have not
> you done that, and handed to Him the bunch minus that key? He gave
> it back, and said He could not be King at all if He could not be King
> of everything. I put my hand in my pocket where I had hidden it, and
> said, "I cannot give it, but You may take it," and He took that tiny key.*
>
> *My King! I see Him now as He stood at the foot of the drawbridge
> of my heart. I see Him radiant as He stood then, for He is here now.
> He looked at me with those eyes which are as a flame of fire, and said,
> "Are all the keys there?" I said, "All but this, and I cannot give it; but
> I am willing for Thee to take it," and He took it at that. Then they
> were all His.*

I remember vividly that evening in early September 1971 when I knelt by an old vinyl sofa at the end of the hallway of my dormitory. There, as best I could, I gave Christ all the keys to my heart. I told Him I was willing to be willing to be His alone. I wasn't sure I was willing; but I knew I was willing to *be* willing. I've never regretted that decision for a moment, and I've never been the same since that moment.

He wants to be our Governor—the head of the government of our hearts and of our homes. Does He hold that rightful place in your life?

❦

The kingdoms of the heathen folk
The Lord shall have therefore;
And he shall be their Governor
And King for evermore.

—THOMAS STERNHOLD, MID-1500S

THE SON

But to the Son He says:
"Your throne, O God, is forever and ever."

—Hebrews 1:8

THE GREATEST IMPONDERABLE OF CHRISTIANITY IS THE Trinity. How can there be one God who eternally exists in three persons? We can observe the reality of it in Scripture and we can formulate it in our theology, but we can never really understand it.

In calling Jesus Christ the Son of God, the Bible in no way diminishes His divinity. He is God Himself. Totally God. Completely God. Forever God. Yet within the Godhead, He voluntarily submits to the Father in terms of His role and function in the universe.

In the early days of the church, there was a man named Arius, a church leader in Alexandria, Egypt, in the fourth century. He was a tall, thin, brilliant man who began teaching that Jesus Christ was the Creator of the world, but that He Himself was a creature of God and not truly divine. The ensuing controversy nearly tore the church apart.

In AD 325, about three hundred church leaders from around the world gathered in the city of Nicea (modern Turkey) to discuss this issue. The total number in the conference, including visitors and observers, was probably about fifteen hundred to two thousand; and some of those in attendance showed the marks of torture from recent persecutions. The creed hammered out at this conference is among the most important documents of the church, affirming that Jesus Christ is not only the Son of God, He is God the Son. It says in part:

We believe in one God, the Father Almighty, Maker of all things visible and invisible. And in one Lord Jesus Christ, the Son of God, begotten of the Father, Light of Light, very God of very God, begotten, not made, being of one substance with the Father; by whom all things were made; who for us men, and for our salvation, came down and was incarnate and was made man; He suffered, and the third day He rose again, ascended to heaven; from thence He comes to judge the living and the dead. And in the Holy Ghost.

At a later conference, held in Chalcedon in AD 451, the dual nature of Jesus was stated even more clearly: "We unanimously teach one and the same Son, our Lord Jesus Christ, complete as to His Godhead, and complete as to His manhood; truly God, and truly man."

We still can't fully understand it; but it helps us to repeat its truth: "But to the Son He says: / 'Your throne, O God, is forever and ever.'"

Jesus! the Name high over all,
In hell or earth or sky;
Angels and men before it fall,
And devils fear and fly.

—CHARLES WESLEY, 1749

THE SON OF ABRAHAM

*The book of the genealogy of Jesus Christ, the Son of David,
the Son of Abraham.*

—MATTHEW 1:1

A PROFESSOR IN BIBLE COLLEGE TOLD US THAT THE DIVI-sion between Genesis 11 and Genesis 12 was greater in importance than the division between the Old and New Testaments. The more I study the Bible, the more I'm convinced he was right. In the first eleven chapters of Genesis, God dealt with the whole earth en masse: The creation. The family of Adam. The flood of Noah. The tower of Babel. God repeatedly demonstrated that the earth as a whole was bent toward corruption and destruction. The word *earth* occurs ninety-two times in Genesis 1–11.

Starting in Genesis 12, however, God launched a brilliant plan to provide redemption for all humanity. He chose one man—Abraham—and gave Him a set of seven remarkable promises. As we read through the Bible, these promises unfold like forest ferns until all the realities of God's redemption are revealed. In His covenant with Abraham, God promised:

1. I will show you a land.

2. I will make you a nation.

3. I will bless you.

4. I will make your name great.

5. I will bless those who bless you.

6. I will curse those who curse you.

7. In you will all the nations of the world be blessed.

From Abraham came Isaac, Jacob, and the nation of Israel—a chosen people. But chosen for what? To bear the Messiah who would provide redemption for all the earth. Paul explained it like this in Galatians 3:

> The Scripture [the Old Testament] foresaw . . . and announced the gospel in advance to Abraham: "All nations will be blessed through you." . . . The promises were spoken to Abraham and to his seed. The Scripture does not say "and to seeds," meaning many people, but "and to your seed," meaning one person, who is Christ. (vv. 8, 16–17 NIV)

God's concern was always for the whole earth, but His chosen method of redemption was a man—Abraham—and to bring from that man a nation, from that nation a Messiah, and from that Messiah a church who would then be sent to all the earth with the good news of forgiveness and eternal life.

It was all planned in advance, from the beginning. That's why the Jews were God's "chosen people," and that's why the very first verse of the New Testament says: "Jesus Christ . . . the Son of Abraham."

The God of Abraham praise, Who reigns enthroned above;
Ancient of everlasting days, and God of Love;
Jehovah, great I AM! by earth and Heav'n confessed;
I bow and bless the sacred Name forever blessed.

—THOMAS OLIVERS, C. 1765

THE SON OF DAVID

And all the multitudes were amazed and said,
"Could this be the Son of David?"

—MATTHEW 12:23

MATTHEW, MARK, AND LUKE ASCRIBE THIS TITLE TO JESUS seventeen times, and the concept behind it opens and closes the New Testament:

—◌ *Matthew 1:1:*

"*The book of the genealogy of Jesus Christ, the Son of David.*"

—◌ *Revelation 22:16:*

"*I am the Root and the Offspring of David, the Bright*
and Morning Star."

It harkens back to the promise God gave to David, which we sometimes call the Davidic Covenant, found in 2 Samuel 7. After David was established on the throne of Israel, he longed to build a dwelling place for God, a house of worship to replace the tattered tabernacle. But as he laid his plans for the temple, the Lord sent him a message through Nathan the prophet:

> *When your days are fulfilled and you rest with your fathers, I will set*
> *up your seed after you, who will come from your body, and I will es-*
> *tablish his kingdom. . . . And I will establish the throne of his king-*
> *dom forever. . . . And your house and your kingdom shall be*
> *established forever before you. Your throne shall be established for-*
> *ever. (2 Sam. 7:12–13, 16)*

Scores of affirmations followed up this promise throughout the remainder of the Old Testament. Isaiah 9:7 says, for example: "Of the increase of His government and peace, / There will be no end, / Upon the throne of David and over His kingdom." Thus do the Hebrew

---

His Sonship Names

Scriptures painstakingly follow the seed of David down through the centuries until the dawning of the New Testament era.

We sometimes think of the Old Testament as a history of the Jewish people, but it would be more accurate to say that it is primarily the history of *one family* within the annals of the Hebrews, one lineage, one branch of the tree. It is the story of the very line of descent of our Lord Jesus Christ, the Son of David, the child from Bethlehem, the Shepherd-King.

The whole Bible is the story of Jesus, first to last, front to back. His lineage unfolds frontward then is traced backward, back through the line of David, back to Abraham, and even back to Adam. As someone once said: "The whole Bible is simply Jesus in print." O great Son of David, You are the King of Israel! You are the King of our hearts, too.

Thou art the King of Israel,
Thou David's royal Son,
Who in the Lord's Name comest,
The King and Blessèd One.

All glory, laud and honor,
To Thee, Redeemer, King,
To Whom the lips of children
Made sweet hosannas ring.

—THEODULPH OF ORLEANS, C. 820

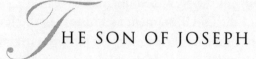

THE SON OF JOSEPH

Philip found Nathanael and said to him, "We have found Him of whom Moses in the law, and also the prophets, wrote—Jesus of Nazareth, the son of Joseph."

—JOHN 1:45

ONE THING INTRIGUES ME MORE THAN ANY OTHER ABOUT the earthly father of Jesus: why did God deliberately keep Joseph in a tortured place for so long? Matthew 1:18–20 says:

> *This is how the birth of Jesus Christ came about: His mother Mary was pledged to be married to Joseph, but before they came together, she was found to be with child through the Holy Spirit. Because Joseph her husband was a righteous man and did not want to expose her to public disgrace, he had in mind to divorce her quietly.*
>
> *But after he had considered this, an angel of the Lord appeared to him in a dream and said, "Joseph son of David, do not be afraid to take Mary home as your wife, because what is conceived in her is from the Holy Spirit. (NIV)*

The angel Gabriel had appeared to Mary before her pregnancy, imparting details of her supernatural conception. Joseph received no such word. No angel whispered the secret in his ear. No cherub tipped him off. Joseph just went happily on his way, head-over-heels in love, until the jolting day when he realized Mary had become impregnated—but not by him.

Joseph must have taken many lonely walks in the hills outside Nazareth, cursing his fate, angry at the Lord, trying to get a grip on his emotions and control his reactions. It was only after he had suffered deep emotional pain that God dispatched an angel to explain things to him. Notice those words: "But *after* he had considered this, an angel of the Lord appeared to him in a dream and said . . ." (Matt. 1:20, italics mine).

God sometimes uses emotional pain to test and train us. I'm sure he was testing Joseph, seeing how he would react. And he was teaching Joseph to lean on Him when all else failed. He was drawing out Joseph's faith and deepening his soul. God was preparing him to be the earthly father of the heavenly King.

If you're suffering emotional pain just now, recognize that God is testing you and training you. And He must have some great work for you to do.

Where Joseph plies his trade, lo, Jesus labors, too;
The hands that all things made an earthly craft pursue,
That weary men in Him may rest,
And faithful toil through Him be blessed.

—WILLIAM HOW, 1872

THE SON OF MAN

The Son of man.

—JOHN 3:13

JESUS OCCASIONALLY REFERRED TO HIMSELF AS SON OF GOD, a title that said, "I am God," but He more often called Himself "Son of Man." In so doing, He was reminding us that He is now—since His miraculous conception—a full-fledged member of the human race. Though sinless, He was and is fully human, subject to the pains and emotions and experiences that are universal to us all. The phrase "Son of Man" was our Lord's favorite title for Himself, appearing eighty-four times in the four Gospels.

In his devotional book *Morning and Evening,* published over a century ago, Charles Haddon Spurgeon said: "How constantly our Master used the title, the 'Son of Man'! If He had chosen, He might always have spoken of Himself as the Son of God, the Everlasting Father, the Wonderful, the Counselor, the Prince of Peace; but behold the lowliness of Jesus! He prefers to call Himself the Son of Man. Let us learn a lesson of humility from our Savior; let us never court great titles or proud degrees."[10]

The wonder of God-made-man is mind-boggling, and we shouldn't become too used to it. C. S. Lewis once said, "If you want to get the hang of it (the incarnation), think how you would like to become a slug or a crab."[11]

Or you could just think of Christ more nearly as He was. Several years ago, I was touring Israel in the early springtime. We were only able to devote a single day to the hillsides of Galilee, and it was a cold, wet, rainy one. There I stood in my raincoat, trying to give a brief devotional, drenched, shivering, my shoes soggy, my spirits soaked, my tour group bravely shielding themselves with an assortment of small umbrellas. I felt miserable. *Why couldn't it have been pretty today?* I asked myself.

Then it hit me. All the Sunday School pictures of Jesus I'd seen in childhood showed Him on bright, sun-splashed days. I don't think I ever saw a depiction of Christ trying to minister in the rain, shivering in the cold, or sloshing through the mud.

But He did. Galilee is cold in the winter, and it's often wet in the spring. Our Lord had stood in the rain just where I was standing. He had shivered just as I was. His feet had been wet, His clothing soaked, His whole body aching for a warm fire or a hot bath. On that Galilee hillside, I saw Jesus more humanly than I ever had before, and somehow I realized afresh that He is the Son of Man, perfectly accessible to both my imagination and to my very soul.

Visualize Him standing just where you are right now, human, close, accessible—the Son of Man.

Beautiful Savior! Lord of all the nations!
Son of God and Son of Man!
Glory and honor, praise, adoration,
Now and forever more be Thine.

—GERMAN JESUITS, 1600S

THE SON OF GOD

So when the centurion and those with him, who were guarding Jesus, saw the earthquake and the things that had happened, they feared greatly, saying, "Truly this was the Son of God!"

— MATTHEW 27:54

THIS IS A CLASSIC TITLE FOR JESUS, BUT MANY OF US UNDER-estimate its meaning because we don't hear those three words —*Son of God*— as they were understood in Bible times. We take them literally, but among the Hebrews it was an idiomatic phrase. They often thought of *father* and *son* as relating not to lineage, but to characteristics. To say "son of . . ." was to mean "possessing the characteristics of."

For example, Genesis 4 describes two brothers, Jabal and Jubal. Jabal became the "father of those who dwell in tents and have livestock" (v. 20), and Jubal became the "father of all those who play the harp and flute" (v. 21). In other words, Jabal was the first rancher, and Jubal was the first musician.

The builders of the tower of Babel were called "sons of men" because they were exhibiting the worst of human behavior. Ministerial students in the Old Testament were called "sons of the prophets." In the Gospels, Jesus referred to James and John as "sons of thunder" because of their volatile tempers (Gen. 11:5; 2 Kings 2:3; Mark 3:17).

When our Lord called Himself the "Son of Man," He was stressing His humanity. When He called Himself the "Son of God," He was emphasizing His deity. He wasn't saying that He was less than God or a product or prodigy of God. He was claiming to be God Himself!

It was a message His Jewish audience couldn't miss. The Gospel of John makes this clear: "Therefore the Jews sought all the more to kill Him, because He not only broke the Sabbath, but also said that God was His Father, making Himself equal with God" (John 5:18).

Making Himself equal with God! Possessing all the characteristics of God! Being God! That's the significance of the phrase. It was nothing less than a claim to divinity. The Son of God, simply put, is rightly called God the Son.

Crown Him the Son of God, before the worlds began,
And ye who tread where He hath trod, crown Him the Son of Man;
Who every grief hath known that wrings the human breast,
And takes and bears them for His own, that all in Him may rest.

—GODFREY THRING, 1874

THE SON OF THE LIVING GOD

*Simon Peter answered and said, "You are the Christ,
the Son of the living God."*

—MATTHEW 16:16

ON SEVERAL OCCASIONS, I'VE THE OPPORTUNITY OF TRAVEL-
ing to the very place where this story occurred. Caesarea Philippi
(modern Banias), is high above the Sea of Galilee, in the mountains
near the headwaters of the Jordan River. There, on the lower slopes of
Mount Hermon, Jesus took His disciples to test them as to His identity.

This area of caves and grottos was a popular center for cultish worship. The ragged terrain coupled with the superstitious nature of
local inhabitants made it a center of pagan rites.

It was especially known for the worship of the Greek god Pan. The
very name of the town, Banias, is a corruption of the English term for
Pan. Pan was the god of the mountainside, of pastures, goats, and
sheep. He was depicted as a shaggy wildman with goat-like horns
and hooves. He had a dark side and often spent his time chasing after
the nymphs of the woods. He was not above mayhem and rape. He
was irritable and cranky, so travelers in wooded areas moved quietly
so as not to disturb him.

From this we get our English word *panic*, and Pan came to be
thought of as the god of anxiety and fright.

How interesting that Jesus of Nazareth took His followers to that
very region to teach them who He really was. This incident marks the
dividing point of our Lord's ministry. Until then, the focus had been
on His *person*. From that point onward, He began teaching them of
His great *work* on the cross. Shortly after Peter confessed Jesus as "the
Christ, the Son of the Living God," we read, "From that time Jesus
began to show to His disciples that He must go to Jerusalem . . . and
be killed, and be raised the third day" (Matt. 16:21).

Our Lord took the disciples to a place of panic to teach them the wonders of His own person and work. He often teaches us our greatest lessons in places of fear and disease. He is greater than Pan, greater than anxiety, greater than superstition, and greater than any false gods.

We find our peace in Him and in His finished work on Calvary. We must choose every day whether we're going to give in to panic or follow Christ, the Son of the Living God.

With us Thou art assembled here,
But O Thyself reveal!
Son of the living God, appear!
Let us Thy presence feel.

—CHARLES WESLEY, 1749

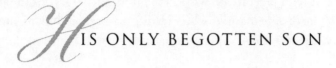

HIS ONLY BEGOTTEN SON

For God so loved the world that He gave His only begotten Son, that whoever believes in Him should not perish but have everlasting life.

—JOHN 3:16

WHAT DOES THE PHRASE "ONLY BEGOTTEN" MEAN? THIS phrase occurs five times in the writings of the apostle John, always about Jesus. But the English term descends from a poorly rendered translation of earlier times.

The original word in the Greek is *monogenous. Mono* means "one," but the stem word, *genous,* is more difficult to figure out. It seems to be more closely related to the idea of "kind" than to that of "origin." In other words, Jesus is the only one of His kind. He's the one and only. The Old Latin translated it as *unicus,* the word from which we get our English word "unique."

Jesus is simply incomparable.

Only Jesus lived so pure and sinless a life that His condemner said, "I find no fault in this Man," and His executioner said, "Truly this Man was the Son of God!" (Luke 23:4, Mark 15:39).

Only Jesus lived so simple and serene a life that the sound of His voice heals human hearts, yet so strong and spectacular a life that the power of His Name alters human history.

Only Jesus turned a localized ministry into a globalized mission that has liberated slaves, educated children, orchestrated charity, postulated truth, and renovated character for two thousand years.

Only Jesus has a name that poets immortalize, saints canonize, demons recognize, foes criticize, and followers personalize as their own—Christ's ones, Christ-ians.

Who else decrees truth, demands obedience, denounces sin, destroys strongholds, delivers hope, delights children, and deposits eternal life in the human soul?

Who else could tie Scripture together with the ribbon of His own identity, fulfilling in Himself every syllable of the world's greatest book? Who else could rise from the dead before the news of His demise could be printed? Who but Jesus could split human history into BC and AD and hold sway over the ages?

There's no one like Him — the Only Begotten of the Father.

God the Father's only Son,
And with Him in glory One,
One in wisdom, One in might,
Absolute and infinite;
Jesu, I believe in thee,
Thou art Lord and God to me.

—SAMUEL J. STONE, 1866

THE CARPENTER'S SON

He taught them in their synagogue, so that they were astonished and said, "Where did this Man get this wisdom and these mighty works? Is this not the carpenter's son?"

—MATTHEW 13:54–55

HE DIDN'T GROW UP IN BOARDING SCHOOLS, ELITE ACAdemies, or royal palaces. His was the carpenter's home, in Nazareth. "Fit place for Jesus," wrote an olden Puritan, "for He had to make a ladder to reach from earth to heaven."

Our Lord's earthly father, Joseph, was a carpenter who evidently died at some point between our Lord's twelfth and thirtieth years; and we can assume Jesus Himself took over His father's business. In Matthew 13:55, He is called "the carpenter's son," but in Mark 6:3, people said of Him, "Is this not the carpenter?"

His hands were rough and leathery. His skin bronzed. His muscles strong. His eye precise. His days long. His craftsmanship superb. His accounts honest.

The irony is too poignant to have been accidental. The tools of His trade became the instruments of His death. Hammer and nails and wood—those were the implements Jesus handled every single day. He used them to build things that lasted.

And so on the cross He took the hammer and nails and wood, using them to erect something that would outlast the ages. "I will build my church," He said, "and all the powers of hell will not conquer it" (Matt. 16:18 NLT).

It's also comforting to know that the Carpenter of Nazareth is working on you and me. We are His construction projects. He has a blueprint for our lives, and He is building us up in the most holy faith. As someone said, "Don't be discouraged. God isn't finished with me yet." Scripture says, "He who has begun a good work in [us] will carry it on to completion" (Phil. 1:6).

Jesus never leaves His projects half-finished.

Have ye been to Nazareth,
Lowly, yet so fair?
Yes, we sought His humble town,
Found our Master there!
Did He dwell in palace fair,
Holding kingly sway?
Nay, we found a Carpenter,
Toiling day by day!

—ELSIE D. YALE, 1921

THE ROCK

He is like a man building a house, who dug deep and laid the foundation on the rock. And when the flood arose, the stream beat vehemently against that house, and could not shake it, for it was founded on the rock.

—LUKE 6:48

ROCK SOLID. GRANITE TOUGH. FIRM AS A STONE. STEADY AS Gibraltar. That's the way we should be at the bases of our lives, in the deepest, most settled places of our hearts.

In this passage, Jesus was concluding His Sermon on the Mount by comparing our lives to houses needing strong foundations. He likened Himself and His teachings to a rock on which we can build with confidence.

I recall reading that several years ago when President Bill Clinton was planning to visit Central America, the Nicaraguan president, Arnoldo Aleman, hurriedly built a new housing complex for hundreds of his poorest citizens. He wanted to impress the American leader. Shortly thereafter, Hurricane Mitch hit the area. The ground didn't provide an adequate foundation for the hastily constructed houses, and two thousand people were drowned, crushed, and scraped to death when their houses were swept away in mudslides. Today all that remains is a field of weeds, some metal crosses, and a few handwritten memorials.

On the other hand, a recent story in a Midwestern newspaper reported on construction of a $9.5 million high school in Hollister, Missouri. Workers unexpectedly discovered a rock plateau just beneath the surface of the fairly level sight. "There's nowhere you can look where you're not hitting rock," said the local school superintendent. Residents now brag their school's firm foundation is symbolic of the educational foundation they want to give their children.

Jesus taught the importance of having a spiritual foundation to our lives, that *strength of foundation* equals *quality of life*. Without the right foundation, no structure is safe. No matter how impressive a building appears above ground, it's what is below the surface and out of sight that counts.

Christ is the Cornerstone, the Sure Foundation, the Rock of Ages. Some people build their lives on friendship, on fads and fashion, on materialism and money, on an altruistic purpose or a selfish dream. There are many footings, but only one Rock. There are many foundations, but only one that will never erode.

～

Some build their hopes on the ever drifting sand,
Some on their fame, or their treasure, or their land;
Mine's on a Rock that forever will stand,
Jesus, the "Rock of Ages."

—TULLIUS C. O'KANE, 1871

THE CHIEF CORNERSTONE

*The stone which the builders rejected has
become the chief cornerstone.*

—PSALM 118:22

THE EIGHTEENTH-CENTURY GERMAN THEOLOGIAN, JOHANN David Michaelis, felt this passage in Psalm 118 was referring to an event that, according to Jewish tradition, took place during the building of Solomon's temple on Jerusalem's Temple Mount. There was reportedly no sound of hammers or saws or pounding of any kind, and the temple was erected in relative silence. The plans were so exact that each stone was shaped perfectly before it left the quarry. Arriving at the temple site, each fit perfectly into its proper place.

But as the stones arrived for the foundation, there was one huge stone, shaped to exacting dimensions, that didn't seem to fit. The builders couldn't find it in their blueprints, so they placed it over to the side. By and by as more stones arrived, it got in the way of the others, and some workmen pushed it over the bank and it rolled into the Kidron Valley.

After the temple's foundation had been laid, the time came to hoist the cornerstone into place. A request was sent to the quarry, but the masons sent back word that they had already delivered it. It was that extra stone that had been ignored and pushed into the valley. It was retrieved and it slid perfectly into place, serving as the stone that held all the others in position.

"The stone which the builders rejected / Has become the chief cornerstone."

Whether the tradition is correct, I don't know. As a prophecy regarding Christ, however, there can be no doubt. Philosophically, He's the only foundation for sound living. Morally, He's the only foundation for clean living. Emotionally, He's the only foundation for happy living. Relationally, He's the only foundation for harmonious living.

Intellectually, He's the only foundation for healthy thinking. Vocationally, He's the only foundation for lasting success. Spiritually, He's the only foundation for eternal life.

Many have rejected Him, but He's the Cornerstone of my life. And yours?

Christ Jesus is the Ground of faith,
Who was made flesh and suffered death;
All that confide in Him alone
Are built on this chief Cornerstone.

—ANONYMOUS GERMAN HYMN, 1791

A STONE FOR A FOUNDATION

Behold, I lay in Zion a stone for a foundation,
A tried stone, a precious cornerstone, a sure foundation.

—ISAIAH 28:16

IN THIS PASSAGE, ISAIAH WAS WARNING THE NATIONAL LEADERS of Judah against becoming enamored with the false gods of surrounding nations. He was contrasting the solidity of faith with the quicksand of compromise. The priests and prophets of Judah were acting like drunken fools, preaching their sodden visions as though ordained by God (v. 7).

Recognizing the true God as the Creator, Sustainer, and Redeemer would provide the intellectual context they needed for wisdom. The stone He laid in Zion would provide that nation with a solid foundation. It would be a tried stone, a precious cornerstone, and a sure footing.

It was a messianic prediction referring to Jesus.

Based on this passage, we can be sure of several things:

Jesus is the foundation of sound decisions. Notice how Isaiah 28:16 ends: "Whoever believes will not act hastily." Those who know Jesus as Savior make careful, prayerful, thoughtful decisions. They don't act impulsively, for they know their normal human impulses are usually wrong.

Jesus is the foundation of inner confidence. When this verse is quoted in the New Testament, there's a different emphasis on that last phrase. Its three appearances in the writings of Paul and Peter (Rom. 9:33, 10:11; 1 Pet. 2:6) say that whoever believes in Him *will not be ashamed*. We don't draw our optimism and cheerfulness in life from the headlines or happenings of the day, from the fortunes or misfortunes that befall us, or from sanguine personalities. They are based on our sure foundation: Jesus Christ. He undergirds us.

Jesus is the foundation of perpetual hope. The passage says, "Behold, I lay in Zion a stone for a foundation," which reminds us immediately of Hebrews 11:10: "[Abraham] waited for a city which has foundations, whose builder and maker is God." Jesus is the founder and builder of the heavenly Jerusalem described in the last two chapters of the Bible. He is preparing a place for us (John 14:2).

The old-timers used to define wisdom as "sanctified common sense," a quality rarely seen today. When our lives are built solidly on Christ, we're people known for our clear thinking, inner confidence, and perpetual hope.

Christ is the sure Foundation the builder did reject,
But He for our salvation is precious and elect
And made the Corner-stone on which the Church is founded;
This marvel now is sounded, the work of God alone.

—ANDERS C. ARREBO, 1623

THE FLINTY ROCK

Who led you through that great and terrible wilderness, in which were fiery serpents and scorpions and thirsty land where there was no water; who brought water for you out of the flinty rock.

—DEUTERONOMY 8:15

CHRIST IS OUR ROCK IN MULTIPLE WAYS. FIRST, HE IS A foundation for our lives. Second, He's our hiding place like a mountain cleft. Third, He's the source of reviving waters of hope and eternal life, as we see in this passage. In Deuteronomy 8, Moses was harkening back to an incident described in Exodus 17:

The LORD said to Moses, "Go on before the people, and take with you some of the elders of Israel. Also take in your hand your rod with which you struck the river, and go. Behold, I will stand before you there on the rock in Horeb; and you shall strike the rock, and water will come out of it, that the people may drink. And Moses did so in the sight of the elders of Israel. (vv. 5–6)

Centuries later, the apostle Paul declared, "And that Rock was Christ" (1 Cor. 10:4).

The Lord commanded Moses, "Strike the rock!" And Moses lifted high his rod—the rigid, inflexible rod of the lawgiver—and with all his might brought it down against the rock in the presence of the elders of Israel. It was a powerful, visual preview of what would happen on Mount Golgotha fourteen hundred years later when the rod of the law struck Christ, the Solid Rock, in the presence of the leaders of Israel.

Somehow this Rock became a fountainhead of waters that quenched the thirst and saved millions of lives.

Jesus told a woman in Samaria, "If you knew the gift of God and who it is that asks you for a drink, you would have asked him and he would have given you living water" (John 4:10 NIV). At the Feast of

Tabernacles, Jesus cried, "If anyone is thirsty, let him come to me and drink. Whoever believes in me, as the Scripture has said, streams of living water will flow from within him" (John 7:37 NIV).

At the end of the Bible, in Revelation 22:17, we have this final invitation to come to Jesus Christ: "The Spirit and the bride say, 'Come!' . . . And let him who thirsts come. Whoever desires, let him take of the water of life freely." It's water from the Rock of our salvation.

O tremble, earth, before the Lord,
In presence of Jehovah fear,
Beneath Whose touch the flinty rock
Became a fount of water clear.

—THE PSALTER, 1912

THE STONE CUT WITHOUT HANDS

Inasmuch as you saw that the stone was cut out of the mountain without hands, and that it broke in pieces the iron, the bronze, the clay, the silver, and the gold—the great God has made known to the king what will come to pass after this.

—DANIEL 2:45

IN THE SECOND CHAPTER OF DANIEL, GOD GAVE NEBUCHAD-nezzar, king of Babylon, a prophetic dream that serves as the framework for all the predictions of Scripture regarding the end times. Using the imagery of a great statue, the Lord forecast the rise and fall of a sequence of empires on the earth—Babylon, Persia, Greece, Rome—followed by an interval for the age of the church, the age of spreading of the gospel to the ends of earth. There would then arise a resurrected Roman Empire, dominated by a mighty man of evil—the Antichrist.

Nebuchadnezzar then saw "a stone . . . cut without hands, which struck the image on its feet of iron and clay, and broke them in pieces. . . . And the stone that struck the image became a great mountain and filled the whole earth" (vv. 34–35).

That image represents Christ and His kingdom. *The Bible Knowledge Commentary* put it this way:

> *In Scripture, a rock often refers to Jesus Christ, Israel's Messiah. God, who had enthroned Nebuchadnezzar and would transfer authority from Babylon to Medo-Persia, then to Greece, and ultimately to Rome, will one day invest political power in a King who will rule over the earth, subduing it to His authority, thus culminating God's original destiny for man.*[12]

The transformation of the stone into a mountain is symbolic of Christ's authority expanding to kingdom levels at the culmination of history.

I often come back to the writings of Daniel when I'm discouraged about politics, headlines, and the current affairs of my nation and world. Things may get worse before they get better. Empires rise and fall. Political parties come and go. Wars and rumors of wars rumble across the earth. But Jesus Christ will one day strike the politics of earth like a colossal Rock demolishing a hideous statue. To Him belong the kingdom and the power and the glory forever.

Down in the feet of iron and of clay,
Weak and divided, soon to pass away;
What will the next great, glorious drama be?
Christ and His coming, and eternity.

—FRANKLIN E. BELDEN, 1886

THE STONE WITH SEVEN EYES

"Behold, I am bringing forth My Servant, the BRANCH.
For behold, the stone
That I have laid before Joshua:
Upon that stone are seven eyes.
Behold, I will engrave its inscription," says the LORD of hosts,
"And I will remove the iniquity of that land in one day."

—ZECHARIAH 3:8–9

ZECHARIAH'S BOOK APPEARS NEAR THE END OF THE OLD
Testament, and it's like a miniature book of Revelation, full of strange
visions and wondrous prophecies. In chapter 3, Zechariah saw the
high priest of Israel, Joshua, dressed in dirty clothes, standing before
the Lord in heaven. Satan was at his right hand, accusing him. But
the Lord said to Satan, "The LORD rebuke you, Satan! . . . Is this not
a brand plucked from the fire?" (v. 2). God then clothed Joshua in
elegant robes.

Satan, the accuser of the brethren, delights in reminding us of past
failures. He knows he can destroy our morale and self-image by
showing us what miserable sinners we've been. But God rebukes
him, for our sins have been nailed to the cross of Christ.

Then the Lord reassured Joshua and gave him a great prophecy
concerning the Messiah who would remove the iniquity of the land in
a single day. This could be a reference to our Lord's death on Calvary,
or it could refer to His second coming.

As noted, Zechariah 3:9 says,

"For behold, the stone
That I have laid before Joshua:
Upon that stone are seven eyes.
Behold, I will engrave its inscription," says the LORD of hosts,
"And I will remove the iniquity of that land in one day."

Let me paraphrase it like this: "Joshua, you feel badly about your sins and Satan has been beating up on you. But I'm giving you a priceless gift you can carry with you everywhere. It's a jewel, a diamond, the most precious stone on earth. See its seven facets. It's perfect [seven is the number of perfection], and on it I have engraved a message about the totality of My forgiveness."

That precious Stone with Seven Eyes is Christ. Whenever Satan troubles you, gaze upon that perfect Jewel and read the inscription, for Jesus came to cleanse us from all our sins.

He spake to His beloved Son:
'Tis time to take compassion;
Then go, bright Jewel of My crown,
And bring to man salvation;
From sin and sorrow set him free,
Slay bitter death for him, that he
May live with Thee forever.

—MARTIN LUTHER, 1523

THE FAITHFUL WITNESS

Jesus Christ, the faithful witness. . . .

—Revelation 1:5

Once during a crisis, I learned two lessons: (1) we must feed our faith and starve our doubts, and (2) and the best way to feed our faith is to focus it on God's promises. We never face situations for which God has not given us certain promises in advance. The way to overcome adversity is to search the Scriptures for the specific promises that relate to our need, focusing on them with mind and heart, claiming them by faith, and trusting Jesus Christ to be as good as His Word.

He is the Faithful Witness.

This title for Christ occurs in Revelation 1, a chapter that begins: "The Revelation of Jesus Christ, which God gave Him to show His servants—things which must shortly take place. And He sent and signified it by His angel to His servant John, who bore witness to the Word of God, and to the testimony of Jesus Christ" (vv. 1–2).

In other words, the Father gave this last book of the Bible to Jesus, who passed it on to John the apostle on the Island of Patmos, and John relayed it to us. The entire Bible is reliable because Jesus is a credible, believable, Faithful Witness. His Word cannot be broken. It is secure in the heavens.

When I'm troubled, I open the Bible at the spot where I last left off reading, and I plunge in, asking God to give me the word I need for the moment. It's remarkable how a verse, a phrase, a cross-reference, or a sentence will jump out at me. Instead of allowing my mind to obsess about my problem, I'm learning to focus it on the Lord and on His promise.

Samuel Clark wrote:

A fixed, constant attention to the promises, and a firm belief in them, would prevent solicitude and anxiety about the concerns of life. It

would keep the mind quiet and composed in every change, and sup-
port and keep up our sinking spirits under the several troubles of
life. . . . For there is no extremity so great, but there are promises suit-
able to it, and abundantly sufficient for our relief in it.[13]

Why? Because every promise in the Bible was given by our Faithful Witness.

When my faith is faint and sickly,
Or when Satan wounds my mind,
Cordials, to revive me quickly,
Healing med'cines here I find:
To the promises I flee,
Each affords a remedy.

—JOHN NEWTON, 1779

LORD OF LORDS

And He has on His robe and on His thigh a name written:
KING OF KINGS
AND LORD OF LORDS.

—REVELATION 19:16

YESTERDAY A WOMAN WHOSE HUSBAND IS OVERSEAS WITH the military, in a war zone and in great danger, came to see me. He's a new Christian but surrounded by temptations and subject to alcoholism. She hasn't been able to sleep for worrying. As soon as she turns off the light, her imagination goes to work. I referred her to this verse.

In my own struggles with anxiety, nothing has helped me more than fixing my mind on God's sovereignty. The word *sovereign* comes from the prefix *sov,* meaning "over," connected to the word *reign.* Jesus reigns over all. He is Lord of lords. He is always in control.

This title is given to our Lord five times in Scripture:

1. Deuteronomy 10:17:

   For the LORD your God is God of gods and LORD of lords, the
   great God, mighty and awesome.

2. Psalm 136:3:

   Oh, give thanks to the Lord of lords!
   For His mercy endures forever.

3. 1 Timothy 6:15–16:

   He who is the blessed and only Potentate, the King of kings and
   Lord of lords, who alone has immortality, dwelling in
   unapproachable light.

4. Revelation 17:14:

These will make war with the Lamb, and the Lamb will overcome them, for He is Lord of lords.

5. Revelation 19:16:

And He has on His robe and on His thigh a name written:
KING OF KINGS
AND LORD OF LORDS.

God doesn't ordain evil, nor is He the author of sin. He allows disasters to occur and wars to rage, but He is able to turn the tides of history toward their appointed ends; and even those events that frighten us don't catch Him unawares. The sovereignty of God extends to the daily details of our lives. He isn't just concerned about nations, but about sparrows and lilies, widows and orphans, and me and you. He is able to work all things for our good, for He is our Lord of Lords, and He is King over all the kings who will ever wear a crown.

***

Crown Him the Lord of lords, who over all doth reign,
Who once on earth, the incarnate Word, for ransomed sinners slain,
Now lives in realms of light, where saints with angels sing
Their songs before Him day and night, their God, Redeemer, King.

—MATTHEW BRIDGES, 1852

THE LION OF THE TRIBE OF JUDAH

Behold, the Lion of the tribe of Judah, the Root of David,
has prevailed to open the scroll and to loose its seven seals.

—REVELATION 5:5

LIONS ARE MENTIONED 150 TIMES IN SCRIPTURE. SAMSON killed a lion in Judges 14; and in 1 Samuel 17, young David killed a lion that was stalking his sheep. Who could forget Daniel being thrown into the den of lions? King Solomon had statues of lions on the steps to his throne. Peter warned us that Satan is "like a roaring lion" (1 Pet. 5:8).

As the term relates to Jesus, we find Him stationed like a colossal Lion at the front door and back door of Scripture, in both Genesis and Revelation.

In Genesis 49:9–10, the patriarch Jacob bestowed his deathbed blessings on his twelve sons, who were to become the twelve tribes of Israel. He announced that one of those tribes—Judah—would be lion-like, and from that tribe would come the great leader whom he called Shiloh ("Man of Peace"):

> *Judah is a lion's whelp. . . .*
> *He bows down, he lies down as a lion:*
> *And as a lion, who shall rouse him?*
> *The scepter shall not depart from Judah,*
> *Nor a lawgiver from between his feet,*
> *Until Shiloh comes;*
> *And to Him shall be the obedience of the people.*

In the last book of the Bible, this prediction is remembered. Revelation 5:5 describes Jesus Christ as the Lion of the Tribe of Judah.

Samuel Davies, a colonial-era clergyman, was in England raising funds for the College of New Jersey. He was invited to preach before

England's King George II. It's the nature of kings to do as they like and even to whisper during sermons. To the astonishment of the audience, Davies stopped his sermon and spoke directly to King George, saying, "When the lion roars, all the animals in the jungle fall silent; and when the Lord speaks, the kings of the earth shut their mouths."

We should be as aware of the Lord's presence as we are of a lion in our homes; for, as C. S. Lewis said about Aslan (in *The Lion, the Witch, and the Wardrobe*), He is not a tame lion. Visualize the Lion of the Tribe of Judah accompanying you at home and abroad every day.

Hosanna in the highest, all glory everlasting,
The cross and its banner triumphant shall wave;
Hosanna in the highest, all glory everlasting,
The Lion of Judah His people will save.

—FANNY CROSBY

THE AMEN

And to the angel of the church of the Laodiceans write, "These things says the Amen, the Faithful and True Witness, the Beginning of the Creation of God."

—REVELATION 3:14

THE WORD *AMEN* IS THE TYPICAL CLOSER FOR OUR PRAYERS. Most people aren't sure what it means, and fewer still consider it a name for Christ Himself.

The word *amen* is transliterated from both the Hebrew and the Greek, where it is spelled exactly as we see it in English. In other words, the term *amen* is probably the most universal word in the human language, being spoken the same in Hebrew, Greek, and English, and in most other languages.

The original Hebrew term meant "to make firm." It conveys the idea of building, supporting, or propping up. In later Greek usage, it came to refer to a solid foundation and carried the idea of truth. In John's Gospel, when Jesus said, "Verily, verily, I say unto you" (KJV), this was the word used in the Greek: "Amen, amen [truly, truly], I say to you."

When we use it at the end of prayers, hymns, and exclamations of worship, it attests to the truthfulness of what we have said: "This is my true prayer. I agree to this. I attest to its truth. It is so. So be it." When, for example, we end a hymn with a choral "Amen," we are attesting to the truth of what we have sung. When we say "Amen" at a statement another makes, we are ratifying the truthfulness of the speaker's statements.

"Amen" is the last word in the Bible, attesting to the truthfulness of everything that has been said in all sixty-six books of inspired Scripture.

In Revelation 3:14, Jesus Christ calls Himself "the Amen." He is the personification of truth. He confirms, supports, props up, attests to, and lives out exact truth in all its dimensions. His words are very truth itself. He never uttered a lie or ever spoke a mistaken word. All His promises are solid to the core. Heaven and earth will pass away, but His words will endure forever. His very nature is truth, and He is our eternal Amen.

Come, Christians, join to sing. Alleluia! Amen!
Loud praise to Christ our King; Alleluia! Amen!
Let all, with heart and voice, Before His throne rejoice;
Praise is His gracious choice. Alleluia! Amen!

—CHRISTIAN H. BATEMAN, 1843

YOUR FIRST LOVE

Nevertheless I have this against you, that you have left your first love.

—REVELATION 2:4

REMEMBER YOUR FIRST LOVE? NOT YOUR FIRST BOYFRIEND or girlfriend, but that vague but sweet memory in the mists of your earliest thoughts. Perhaps it was your infant-love for the mother who held you snugly, joyfully during your first moments of life.

My mom was fiercely loyal to my cantankerous grandma, defending and caring for her even when others shook their heads in amazement. I finally figured out why. When my mom was born, she was so tiny that the midwife, not expecting her to live, laid her in the crib to die. She apparently weighed no more than three pounds or so. This was in the early 1900s, in Appalachia, in January, in a cold and drafty farmhouse. But my grandmother snapped, "Give me that baby!" and she started nursing her. My mother grew up to be hale and hearty, and she never forgot what she couldn't remember—her first love.

Our first love is the most bonding experience of life, and it's always more special than all the other wonderful "regular loves" we experience in life. Our love for Jesus isn't "regular love." It's a kind of "first love." In fact, the Bible affords Him this special name: "Your First Love." Originally John wrote these words to a church that had a long and storied history as the greatest church of the New Testament era: the church in the city of Ephesus. Founded by Saint Paul, it counted among its pastors the apostle John and the youthful Timothy. In Revelation 2:2–3, Christ commended the church, saying, "I know your works, your labor, your patience, and that you cannot bear those who are evil. And you have tested those who say they are apostles and are not, and have found them liars; and you have persevered and have patience, and have labored for My name's sake."

Yet for all that, they had allowed other motivations to slip into their hearts, marring their all-eclipsing love for Jesus Christ, who should have been first in their hearts, minds, and souls. That's of great concern to Him who gave His life for us. Remember in John 21 how Jesus kept asking His disciple, "Peter, do you love Me?"

Our love for Jesus should guide every decision, drive every ministry, fuel our every service, determine every personal standard, and energize our every service of public worship.

> *Then why, O blessèd Jesus Christ*
> *Should I not love Thee well?*
> *Not for the hope of winning heaven,*
> *Nor of escaping hell.*
>
> *Not with the hope of gaining aught,*
> *Nor seeking a reward,*
> *But as Thyself hast lovèd me,*
> *O everlasting Lord!*
>
> *E'en so I love Thee, and will love,*
> *And in Thy praise will sing,*
> *Solely because Thou art my God,*
> *And my eternal King.*

—ANCIENT LATIN HYMN OF UNKNOWN ORIGIN

HE ALPHA AND THE OMEGA

I am the Alpha and the Omega.

—REVELATION 1:8

THIS TITLE FOR CHRIST IS HIS MONOGRAM, AS IT WERE, implying the all-inclusive nature of His attributes. Alpha is the *A* of the Greek alphabet, and Omega is the *Z*. In English terms, we would say that He is the A and the Z.

Every word that can be uttered, every praise we can speak, every quality we can write, every thought we can conceive, every syllable we can form—He exceeds them all. He is the Author and Finisher of Our Faith. He is the source of our salvation and the destination of our dreams. He is the first cause and the last word. He is the origin of creation and the terminus of time. He reigns from the vanishing point to the vanishing point. From past to future, from everlasting to everlasting, He is God.

This is the New Testament version of the truth found in Psalm 90: "From everlasting to everlasting, You are God." Jesus Christ transcends time and pervades eternity. He appears at the beginning and the end of the ages simultaneously. And consider this: if Christ is at the beginning and ending of history, He's also at the beginning and ending of our lives, present at the moments of our conceptions and on the days of our funerals. He knows how to lead us from birth to death, and He understands the way we should take at every juncture.

Of the Father's love begotten, ere the worlds began to be,
He is Alpha and Omega, He the source, the ending He,
Of the things that are, that have been,
And that future years shall see, evermore and evermore!

At His Word the worlds were framèd; He commanded; it was done:
Heaven and earth and depths of ocean in their threefold order one;
All that grows beneath the shining
Of the moon and burning sun, evermore and evermore!

— Aurelius Prudentius, fifth century

THE RULER OVER
THE KINGS OF THE EARTH

Jesus Christ, the faithful witness, the firstborn from the dead,
and the ruler over the kings of the earth.

—REVELATION 1:5

CHURCHILL, ALEXANDER, CAESAR, KENNEDY, STALIN, CAStro, Hitler, Nebuchadnezzar, Napoleon, Lincoln, Louis the XIV, Henry the VIII, Washington, Lenin, Herod the Great, Jefferson, Constantine I, the legendary Arthur—all of them put together and multiplied a thousand times can never begin to approach the power, popularity, and perpetual reign of the unlettered carpenter of Nazareth.

As an unknown author put it: "I am far within the mark when I say that all the armies that ever marched, all the navies that were ever built, all the parliaments that ever sat and all the kings that ever reigned, put together, have not affected the life of man upon this earth as powerfully as has that one solitary life."

He is Ruler over the kings of the earth.

Napoleon Bonaparte reportedly said:

You speak of Caesar, Alexander, of their conquests; of the enthusiasm they enkindled in the hearts of their soldiers; but can you conceive of a dead man making conquests with an army faithful and entirely devoted to His memory? My army has forgotten me while living.

Alexander, Caesar, Charlemagne and myself have founded empires. But on what did we rest the creations of our genius? Upon force! Jesus Christ alone founded His empire upon love: and at this hour millions of men would die for Him. . . . What an abyss between my deep misery and the eternal reign of Christ who is proclaimed, loved, adored, and whose reign is extending over all the earth.

More than once my heart has skipped a beat when the television screen went momentarily blank and the announcer said, "We interrupt this program for a special news bulletin." An assassination. A death. A bomb. An attack. A war. Every day is uncertain, but over all the crises and chaos of life, He reigns—the Ruler of the kings of the earth. When we are in Christ, we're in good hands.

Shouldn't such a one be the absolute monarch of your life and mine?

North and South shall own Thy sway;
East and West Thy voice obey;
Crowns and thrones before Thee fall,
King of kings and Lord of all.

—Fanny Crosby, u.d.

THE LORD WHO IS AND WHO WAS AND WHO IS TO COME

"I am the Alpha and the Omega, the Beginning and the End," says the Lord, "who is and who was and who is to come, the Almighty."

—REVELATION 1:8

Holy, holy, holy! All the saints adore Thee,
Casting down their golden crowns around the glassy sea;
Cherubim and seraphim falling down before Thee,
Who was, and is, and evermore shall be.

—REGINALD HEBER, 1826

HE IS THE LORD WHO WAS. JESUS WAS. BEFORE THERE WAS anything but nothingness, He existed. In the fading, unfathomable ages of eternity past, He was. When the universe flared into existence, He was, speaking the Word, designing the worlds with all their beauty and the galaxies with all their glitter. Even then, He knew the plans He had for us. He knew us before our births and loved us before we came into being. The Lord said to Jeremiah, "Before I formed you in the womb I knew you; / Before you were born I sanctified you" (Jer. 1:5).

He is the Lord who is. He's alive, present, observant, carefully watching over His children. His eyes never close, His attention never wavers, His love never ceases, and His care never fails. He dwells in the highest heaven, yet He is closer to you than your right hand. "He will not allow your foot to be moved; / He who keeps you will not slumber. / Behold, He who keeps Israel / Shall neither slumber nor sleep" (Ps. 121:3–4).

He is the Lord who is to come. He will be. He encompasses time and transcends eternity. He knows the future as thoroughly as He knows the past, and His guiding Hand is leading us toward His preordained providence. "I know what I'm doing. I have it all planned out—

plans to take care of you, not abandon you, plans to give you the future you hope for" (Jer. 29:11 MESSAGE).

What bothers you most? The past with its failures, regrets, and missed opportunities? The present with its stresses and strains? The future with its uncertainties?

Trust Him with all yesterday, today, and tomorrow. He is Lord of all three days.

The God Who reigns on high the great archangels sing,
And "Holy, holy, holy!" cry, "Almighty King!
Who was, and is, the same, and evermore shall be:
Jehovah—Father—great I AM, we worship Thee!"

—THOMAS OLIVERS, 1765

THE ALMIGHTY

"I am ... the Almighty."

—REVELATION 1:8

THE TERM *ALMIGHTY* OCCURS FIFTY-SEVEN TIMES IN THE Bible, always and only referring to God Himself. He alone possesses all power and might. Theologians use the word *omnipotent* to describe this quality. *Omni* means "all," and *potent* means "might" or "power." It's a term usually applied to God the Father or to the entire Godhead, but here in Revelation 1:8 it describes our Lord Jesus Christ.

Would you like to hazard a guess as to which biblical author most often used the term *Almighty?* Was it John, who wrote the book of Revelation and who gives us such powerful utterances as: "Holy, holy, holy, / Lord God Almighty" (Rev. 4:8)? No, though he did use the word eight times.

Was it the writers of the Psalms, that great Hebrew hymnal at the heart of our Bible? No. Only two occurrences there, the most beautiful being Psalm 91:1: "He who dwells in the secret place of the Most High / Shall abide under the shadow of the Almighty."

Nor was it Paul. He used the term only once, when he was quoting from the Old Testament.

For those who are facing insurmountable problems in life, to know that God possesses total power, that He dispenses His power without in the least diminishing His supply, that His power is as infinite as He Himself is—that is a very comforting thought. We shouldn't be surprised, then, that the patriarch Job, who endured so many waves of disaster and distress, called God by this name thirty-one times—more than all the other Bible writers combined. In his distress, Job repeatedly said, "The Almighty ... The Almighty. ... The Almighty. ..."

He was shipwrecked on God and stranded on omnipotence. And come to think of it, that's not such a bad place to be.

Immortal, invisible, God only wise,
In light inaccessible hid from our eyes,
Most blessèd, most glorious, the Ancient of Days,
Almighty, victorious, Thy great Name we praise.

—WALTER C. SMITH, 1876

A MALE CHILD RULING THE NATIONS

She bore a male Child who was to rule all nations with a rod of iron. And her Child was caught up to God and His throne.

—REVELATION 12:5

THE CHAPTER BEGINS WITH A VIVID DESCRIPTION OF THE birth of a baby who will rule the nations with an iron scepter. The mother is not simply the virgin Mary, but all Israel—a nation great with child, crying in the pain of childbirth, about to bring forth the Messiah.

This is the Nativity story of Christ as presented by the apostle John.

Yet it's a strange picture. Among the cattle, camels, donkeys, and sheep of the stable in Bethlehem lurks a sinister monster. Revelation 12:3 describes a "great, fiery red dragon"—not a typical figure in our Nativity sets.

"The dragon stood before the woman who was ready to give birth, to devour her Child as soon as it was born" (Rev. 12:4). This dragon represents the devil, who was carefully watching the birth of our Lord. It was Satan who sought to destroy the Christ child by moving mad old King Herod to slaughter the boys of Bethlehem.

"She bore a male Child who was to rule all nations with a rod of iron. And her Child was caught up to God and His throne." This refers to the ascension of Christ at the end of His earthly ministry. The devil repeatedly tried to discredit the Messiah. He tried to kill him as a baby. He sought to tempt Him as a man. He aimed to distract Him at every turn. In the end, He sifted the disciples like wheat, gained a foothold in one of them (Judas), and had the Son of God nailed to a cross and sealed in a tomb.

But Christ burst forth, and forty days later, He was snatched up to God and to His throne. One day He will return and rule the nations of earth.

There's much more in Revelation 12 about the troubles and travails of the Jewish people. But the basic message is this: this child—Jesus Messiah—will not be denied. He will not be detoured, defeated, or destroyed. The entire world will one day acknowledge Him and every knee will bow and every tongue confess Him as Lord (Phil. 2:10).

Come in Thy glorious might,
Come with the iron rod,
Scattering Thy foes before Thy face,
Most mighty Son of God!

—HORATIUS BONAR, 1846

THE BRIGHT AND MORNING STAR

"I, Jesus, have sent My angel to testify to you these things in the churches. I am the Root and Offspring of David, the Bright and Morning Star." And the Spirit and the bride say, "Come!"

—REVELATION 22:16–17

GOD PROMISED ABRAHAM HIS DESCENDANTS WOULD BE AS numberless as the stars in the heavens. One star, however, outshines all the rest. Even the false prophet Balaam spoke of it in Numbers 24:17 when he uttered, "I see Him, but not now; / I behold Him, but not near; / A Star shall rise out of Israel."

At the nativity of Christ, it was a star symbolizing His birth that led the Magi to Bethlehem. Peter later explained, "And so we have the prophetic word confirmed, which you do well to heed as a light that shines in a dark place, until the day dawns and the morning star rises in your hearts" (2 Pet. 1:19).

Revelation calls Him the "Bright and Morning Star."

In astronomy, the bright and morning star is not a star at all, but the planet Venus that appears in the eastern sky just before dawn. Because Venus is nearer the sun than we are, it appears brighter and is by far the brightest object in the celestial sky, save the sun and moon.

As it relates to Christ, what does this symbolize? Coming at the end of the book of Revelation, it isn't hard to ascertain the significance of this title. The appearance of the morning star in the dawning sky is a sign that night is nearly over and morning is at hand.

The dark epoch of earth's sinful history is nearly past, like the transitory watches of the night. Soon, the Lord Jesus shall rise from His throne like the star of the morning, ushering in the promised eternal day for His children. Until then, the cry goes out to the entire world:

Come! "The Spirit and the bride say, 'Come!' . . . And let him who thirsts come. Whoever desires, let him take the water of life freely" (Rev. 22:17).

The only Son from Heaven,
Foretold by ancient seers,
By God, the Father, given,
In human shape appears;
No sphere His light confining,
No star so brightly shining
As He, our Morning Star.

—ELISABETHE VON MESERITZ CRUCIGER, 1524

THE WORD OF GOD

He was clothed with a robe dipped in blood, and
His name is called The Word of God.

—REVELATION 19:13

THE RETURN OF CHRIST IS OFT MENTIONED IN SCRIPTURE, and some of the passages are incredibly detailed and dynamic. But the climax of all eschatology is Revelation 19, the second-coming chapter in the Bible, in which the Word of God (Jesus) suddenly appears at closing moments of history.[14] This chapter is filled with vivid symbolism, but its truths are reasonably clear and incredibly heart-lifting.

HIS FIRST COMING	HIS SECOND COMING
LUKE 2	REVELATION 19
He was born to a virgin in poverty	*He will return in a flash of glory*
His birth was announced by angels	*His return is heralded by angels*
The angelic message: A Savior is born	*The angelic message: A Judge has appeared*
His birth was unnoticed	*His omnipotence is proclaimed*
He came alone	*He returns with legions of angels*
Hotels were closed to Him	*Heaven is opened for Him*
Jesus was laid in a manger	*Jesus is mounted on a white horse*
He brings peace on earth, goodwill toward man	*He judges and makes war*

His eyes are closed in a baby's sleep	His eyes are a flame of fire
His head is nestled to a virgin mother	On His head are many crowns
He was wrapped in swaddling cloth	He is clothed in a robe dipped in blood
The armies of Herod pursued Him	The armies of heaven follow Him
Out of His mouth came a baby's soft cry	Out of His mouth comes a sharp sword with which to strike the nations
His name is Jesus, for He shall save His people from their sins	On His robe is written this name: KING OF KINGS AND LORD OF LORDS

Ere the blue heav'ns were stretched abroad,
From everlasting was the Word:
With God He was; the Word was God,
And must divinely be adored.

—ISAAC WATTS, 1707

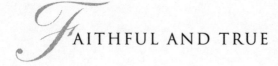

FAITHFUL AND TRUE

Now I saw heaven opened, and behold, a white horse.
And He who sat on him was called Faithful and True.

—REVELATION 19:11

JESUS IS NOT ONLY FAITHFUL AND TRUE, HE IS FAITHFUL and True. That's His middle name. I was thinking of this today as I studied John 4. A governmental official came to Jesus, begging Him to heal his son who was dying. "Sir," said the man, "Come down before my child dies" (v. 49 NIV).

But Jesus had no intention of going with the man. His schedule was planned from eternity past, and it wasn't possible for Him to take the days needed to travel to the man's house. Yet He didn't neglect the man's crisis. He gave him a simple promise: "You may go. Your son will live" (v. 50 NIV).

What would you have done at that point? Jesus sent the man home with nothing more than seven syllables. He didn't accompany him. He didn't offer to visit later. The man turned to leave empty-handed, but not empty-eared; He had a promise spoken by Him who is Faithful and True.

John 4:50 gives one of the best definitions of faith in the Bible when it says, "The man took Jesus at his word and departed" (NIV).

The account continues, "While he was still on the way, his servants met him with the news that his boy was living. When he inquired as to the time when his son had got better, they said to him, 'The fever left him yesterday at the seventh hour.' Then the man realized that this was the exact time at which Jesus had said to him, 'Your son will live'" (vv. 51–52 NIV).

What if the man had returned home anxious, fearful, sad, and uncertain? What if he had worried that Jesus was unfaithful and untrue?

But he took the Lord at His word and returned home, rejoicing

---

that Jesus had the power to do what He had promised. And though the man didn't fully realize it at the time, the answer had already come the moment the promise was spoken.

Do you need to find a promise from Faithful and True for your life today? Let's give our burdens to Him and go on our way with the assurance that the answer has already been granted and will be revealed in His perfect timing.

Come, Thou Conqueror of the nations,
Now on Thy white horse appear;
Earthquakes, famines, desolations
Signify Thy kingdom near:
True and faithful!
Stablish Thy dominion here.

—CHARLES WESLEY, 1759

THE NAME NO ONE KNOWS

His eyes were like a flame of fire, and on His head were many crowns.
He had a name written that no one knew except Himself.

—REVELATION 19:12

YEARS AGO, I DISCOVERED A. W. TOZER'S CLASSIC LITTLE book *The Knowledge of the Holy;* it's a probing assessment of the attributes (qualities) of God. Tozer begins by decrying the low view of God held by many in today's church. "If we would bring back spiritual power to our lives, we must begin to think of God more nearly as He is," he wrote.[15]

That's true, yet by the same token we know that God Himself is truly incomprehensible. He is not like anything. He is "high and lifted up," lofty and veiled in "unapproachable light" (Isa. 6:1; 1 Tim. 6:16). He possesses attributes we can never discover, for He Himself is infinite, inexhaustible, unlimitable, eternal, shoreless, measureless, unplumbed, perpetual, and vastly beyond the reach of human understanding.

As Nicholas of Cusa wrote, "The intellect knoweth that it is ignorant of Thee, because it knoweth Thou canst not be known, unless the unknowable could be known, and the invisible beheld, and the inaccessible attained."

According to most commentators, this is the significance of our Lord's name that cannot be known. Revelation 19 presents a vivid picture of the return of Jesus Christ at the moment of Armageddon. Surrounded by the thunderous songs of the angelic army, He appears through the opened heavens riding a white horse. His eyes "were like a flame of fire, and on His head were many crowns. . . . He was clothed with a robe dipped in blood," and "out of His mouth goes a sharp sword" (vv. 12–13, 15).

Several names are ascribed to the Lord Jesus in this chapter: the Lamb, Jesus, Faithful and True, King of kings, and Lord of lords. But

He also has a name that no one knows. This suggests there are aspects of His character and qualities known only within the Godhead.

We could more easily pour the ocean into a tin can as to try to contain within our finite brains the infinite glories of Jesus Christ. How wonderful to have a Savior-God so vast, so high, so unending, so unfathomable, so worthy of our wonder and worship.

How wonderful, how beautiful,
The sight of Thee must be;
Thy endless wisdom, boundless power,
And glorious purity!

—FREDERICK W. FABER, 1849

THE FAITHFUL AND TRUE WITNESS

These things says the Amen, the Faithful and True Witness,
the Beginning of the creation of God.

—REVELATION 3:14

THE WORDS *FAITHFUL* AND *TRUE* ARE LINKED TOGETHER FIVE
times in the Bible—once in the book of Jeremiah (42:5) and four
times here in Revelation (3:14, 19:11; 21:5; 22:6). Interestingly, there
appears to be a connection between the passage in Jeremiah and those
in Revelation. It seems that the Lord's title in Revelation 3:14—the
True and Faithful Witness—is borrowed from words spoken by
some faithless and fickle characters in Jeremiah's day.

In Jeremiah 42, a handful of panic-stricken citizens approached Jeremiah, seeking God's advice. The Babylonian army had destroyed
Jerusalem and burned down its temple. A scattered group of trauma-
tized survivors asked Jeremiah for guidance, saying, "Please, let our
petition be acceptable to you, and pray for us to the LORD your God,
for all this remnant (since we are left but a few of many, as you can
see), that the LORD your God may show us the way in which we
should walk and the thing we should do" (vv. 2–3).

So far so good. They seemed committed to seeking God's counsel.
They continued: "Let the LORD be *a true and faithful witness* between
us, if we do not do according to everything which the LORD your God
sends us by you. Whether it is pleasing or displeasing, we will obey
the voice of the LORD our God" (vv. 5–6, italics mine).

The Lord waited ten days to send them an answer. He could, of
course, have answered at once; but He was testing their resolve. As it
turned out, their words were cheap. After the ten-day waiting period,
Jeremiah revealed what God commanded them: to remain in the ruined land of Judah and tend it. By then, however, they had decided to

migrate to Egypt where the grass seemed greener, and Jeremiah could not dissuade them from their fatal choice.

Are you disappointed at the fickleness of someone you know? Has he or she proven to be unfaithful and untrue? Has he or she let you down? Perhaps you're upset at your own inconsistencies.

Jesus Christ is the Faithful and True Witness. He doesn't waver in His resolve or forget the promises He's made. He will never disappoint. He isn't fickle, but always faithful, the same yesterday, today, and forever.

Keep your eyes on Him.

O what shall I do my Savior to praise,
So faithful and true, so plenteous in grace,
So strong to deliver, So good to redeem
The weakest believer that hangs upon Him!

—CHARLES WESLEY, 1742

THE FIRSTBORN FROM THE DEAD

And from Jesus Christ, the faithful witness, the firstborn from the dead.

—REVELATION 1:5

MY FATHER, WHO GREW UP IN THE APPALACHIANS, USED TO tell of a disagreeable man who lived farther on up the mountain. His name was Nick Hill, and my dad was afraid of him. He was a threatening, surly man who beat his children and cursed his neighbors.

One night, the Hill family sent an urgent message: Nick was dying. Houses were sparse on that mountain, and the village was two miles away; so my dad's family hurried up to the old Hill place. What they saw left a lasting impression on my father. Nick Hill was convulsing on his bed like a wild man, screaming, his eyes wide in horror, his sons trying to restrain him. And his words blistered the walls of his little wooden house: "Lord God Almighty, boys, hold me down! I see hellfire a'coming!" In a paroxysm of terror, he tumbled into eternity.

Years later, my father himself lay on his deathbed, or so we thought. He later told us that he felt his soul slipping from his body and traveling gently, sweetly, toward Jesus. It was like being drawn into the light. At a certain point, however, the course reversed: he awoke and eventually recovered. He never afterward seemed fearful of death.

Knowing Jesus makes all the difference.

When the Bible refers to Jesus as the "firstborn from the dead," it provides us with a fascinating picture. Just as He is the Firstborn of Mary, entering the world from her womb, so He is the Firstborn of the Grave, entering the world from its tomb.

In other words, the tomb is a womb. Out of the sepulcher comes new life. Out of death comes victory. Out of the grave comes eternity. And because Christ is the Firstborn from the Dead, He has paved the way for you and me. Because He lives, we shall live also. Death isn't a ticket to hell, but a tunnel to heaven; for "to be absent from the body [is] to be present with the Lord" (2 Cor. 5:8).

Again, knowing Jesus makes all the difference, for "He is the head of the body, the church, who is the beginning, the firstborn from the dead, that in all things He may have the preeminence" (Col. 1:18).

Christ Jesus lay in death's strong bands, for our offenses given;
But now at God's right hand He stands, and brings us life from heaven.
Wherefore let us joyful be, and sing to God right thankfully
Loud songs of Alleluia! Alleluia!

—MARTIN LUTHER, 1524

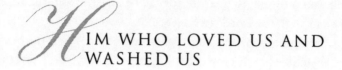
HIM WHO LOVED US AND WASHED US

To Him who loved us and washed us from our sins in His own blood.

—REVELATION 1:5

DR. KARL BARTH, ONE OF THE MOST BRILLIANT THEOLO-gians of the twentieth century, was reportedly asked if he could summarize his complex theology in a simple sentence. Dr. Barth thought a moment, then said: "Jesus loves me, this I know, for the Bible tells me so."

After the publication of my book of hymn stories, *Then Sings My Soul,* I received a letter from a woman in Florida named Sally Offenhauer, who told me about her son.

When Bo was ten years old, he was riding his bicycle in front of their house when he was hit by a truck going fifty miles an hour. Witnesses working on an adjacent roof said the boy flew over power lines, landed on a concrete sewer pad, rolled one hundred feet, and came to rest in the yard across the street.

As they rushed to the hospital in the ambulance, it became clear Bo was going into shock. He was puffy and growing pale. The color drained from his face. His breathing was shallow. Instinctively, Sally and her husband, with Bo in the ambulance, began singing, "Jesus loves me, this I know; / For the Bible tells me so."

Bo's lips began to move, and he began to sing, weakly at first, then more strongly. The color returned to his face, and they could only describe it as miraculous. In the emergency room, the CT scan found no head injuries, no internal injuries, and nothing life-threatening. His major injury was to his knee, which later required a number of surgeries.

But the woman said in the letter to me, "To make a long story short, Bo is now twenty-one and a junior in college. God has put it on

my heart to make certain that every child in the world has an opportunity to learn that life-saving hymn."

It's a miracle truth for everyone on earth. Jesus loves us! "To him
who loved us and washed us from our sins in His own blood . . . be
glory and dominion forever and ever. Amen" (Rev. 1:5–6).

Jesus loves me! This I know,
For the Bible tells me so.
Little ones to Him belong;
They are weak, but He is strong.

—ANNA WARNER, 1860

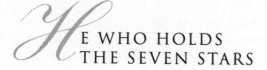

HE WHO HOLDS THE SEVEN STARS

To the angel of the church of Ephesus write,
"These things says He who holds the seven stars in His right hand,
who walks in the midst of the golden lampstands."

—REVELATION 2:1

DON'T BE TOO INTIMIDATED BY THE BOOK OF REVELATION. The very word *revelation,* after all, means "to reveal." The Lord gave us this book on purpose—to show His servants the "things which must shortly take place" (Rev. 1:1). It's the only book in the Bible that both begins and ends with a promise to bless those who study it. It opens by saying, "Blessed is he who reads and those who hear the words of this prophecy, and keep those things which are written in it; for the time is near" (1:3). And it ends with a similar promise: "Blessed is he who keeps the words of the prophecy of this book" (22:7).

One of the great secrets to Revelation is realizing that the book itself interprets much of its own symbolism. For example, what are the seven stars and the golden lampstands mentioned at the beginning of chapter 2? Just read chapter 1! Writing specifically to seven individual churches in Asia Minor (modern Turkey), John described his vision of the exalted Christ: "Having turned, I saw seven golden lampstands, and in the midst of the seven lampstands One like the Son of Man, clothed with a garment down to the feet and girded about the chest with a golden band. . . . He had in His right hand seven stars" (vv. 12–13, 16). Then, coming to the end of chapter 1, we read: "The seven stars are the angels of the seven churches, and the seven lampstands which you saw are the seven churches" (v. 20).

The word *angel* literally means "messenger." Most commentators believe this is referring to the leaders or pastors of the seven churches to which John was writing.

The picture, then, is of our Lord Jesus Christ during this present age, walking among His churches and holding their pastors in His hand. To me, as a pastor, that's a vivid thought. Amid the toil and tears of my work, here is the Savior. He goes with me on my visits. He tutors me in my study. He stands with me in the pulpit. He gives me wisdom for the meetings and encounters that fill my day. And as we worship on Sunday, there He is among His people. We don't have a distant, absent Savior. He's in this very room.

Visualize that, and be encouraged.

Let every lamp be burning bright,
The darkest hour is nearing;
The darkest hour of earth's long night,
Before the Lord's appearing.

—Franklin E. Belden, 1886

THE MINISTER OF
THE SANCTUARY

We have such a High Priest, who is seated at the right hand of the
throne of the Majesty in the heavens, a Minister of the sanctuary
and of the true tabernacle which the Lord erected.

—HEBREWS 8:1–2

ONE DAY SOME YEARS AGO, RETURNING FROM A VIGOROUS overseas trip, I was tired and frustrated. I needed a day of rest, but I had returned to a heavy schedule with a couple of deadlines and several problems. By mid-morning my strength was gone, and so were my spirits. Closing my door, I swept everything off my desk and spent several hours studying an unusual subject in the Bible: the tabernacle, God's tent in the wilderness.

It was like a tonic. I realized afresh the energizing power of this strange subject. Studying the tabernacle brings us face-to-face with our Lord Jesus. The Bible devotes only two chapters to the creation and four chapters to the birth of Christ, but fifty are given over to this wilderness tabernacle (thirteen chapters in Exodus, eighteen in Leviticus, thirteen in Numbers, two in Deuteronomy, and four in Hebrews).

Why such emphasis? Because every detail of the tabernacle points to Jesus Christ. Every aspect teaches some truth about His person and work.

In Hebrews 8:2, the writer called Jesus the Minister of the Sanctuary. Just as Aaron ministered in the earthly tabernacle, so Jesus Christ is our High Priest ministering above, in the heavenly tabernacle, at this very moment.

There's a ministry taking place now invisible to human eyes. Beyond earth's dimensions, powerful spiritual forces are working for your enabling. Our Intercessor is there at this moment with you on His mind, representing you before God and interceding as your personal High Priest. Jesus is the Minister in the Sanctuary, working behind the scenes—above the scenes—every minute of your life. Count on it, and when you grow weary and worn, visualize His present ministry for you.

Before the throne of God above
I have a strong and perfect plea.
A great high Priest whose Name is Love
Who ever lives and pleads for me.

—CHARITIE L. BANCROFT, 1863

A MERCIFUL AND FAITHFUL HIGH PRIEST

In all things He had to be made like His brethren, that He might be
a merciful and faithful High Priest in things pertaining to God,
to make propitiation for the sins of the people.

—HEBREWS 2:17

THE WORD *PRIEST* CONVEYS DIFFERENT IMAGES TO DIFFERENT people, but in its biblical sense it refers to a go-between between heaven and earth. A priest represents our needs to God while at the same time representing God's grace to us. He is an intermediary, a connecting link, a liaison, a mediator. "There's one God and only one, and one Priest-Mediator between God and us—Jesus, who offered himself in exchange for everyone held captive by sin, to set them all free," says 1 Timothy 2:5–6 (MESSAGE).

Hebrews 2:17 offers two adjectives describing Jesus as our High Priest. First, He is *merciful.* This comes from the Greek word *éleos,* which carries the idea of seeing someone's need and having compassion and sympathy for him or her.

The second word is *faithful.* This means that our High Priest is going to keep every single promise and obligation He has made. Can any of our Lord's promises expire before fruition? Joshua 21:45 says: "Not a word failed of any good thing which the Lord had spoken to the house of Israel. All came to pass."

Again we read, "Know in all your hearts and in all your souls that not one thing has failed of all the good things which the Lord your God promised concerning you. All have come to pass for you; not one thing of them has failed" (Josh. 23:14 AMP).

As Solomon dedicated the temple in Jerusalem, he said, "Blessed be the LORD. . . . There has not failed one word of all His good promise, which He promised through His servant Moses" (1 Kings 8:56).

Jesus is your Merciful and Faithful High Priest. He sees you with compassion and keeps all His promises. Live each day secure in that!

Jesus, my great High Priest, offered His blood, and died;
My guilty conscience seeks no sacrifice beside:
His powerful blood did once atone, and now it pleads before the throne.

—ISAAC WATTS, 1709

A PRIEST FOREVER

The LORD has sworn and will not relent,
"You are a priest forever
According to the order of Melchizedek."

—PSALM 110:4

AS SOON AS WE SAY THAT JESUS IS OUR GREAT HIGH PRIEST, we have an interesting biblical problem. According to the Old Testament, Aaron, who was of the tribe of Levi, headed up the Jewish priesthood. In the book of Exodus, God appointed the Levites as the priestly tribe of Israel, and the high priest of Israel was always of the tribe of Levi. Thus was it inscribed with biblical authority.

Jesus, however, was not a Levite. He descended from the tribe of Jacob. How, then, could He fulfill the Old Testament requirements of the priesthood? Psalm 110 anticipated and answered that question a thousand years before His birth.

In Genesis 14, a man named Melchizedek served in the role of priest long before Levi was born. Melchizedek, who lived in the days of Abraham, was a universal priest separate from Levi. In Psalm 110:4, God the Father made this declaration to God the Son: "You are a priest forever / According to the order of Melchizedek."

Not according to the order of Levi, but according to the order of Melchizedek.

The book of Hebrews goes on to explain that Jesus Christ is our High Priest, not in the Jewish line of Levi, for Christ descended from the tribe of Judah, but after the order of Melchizedek. Jesus and Melchizedek make up an exclusive branch of the priesthood.

In fact, if you count them up in Psalm 110 and Hebrews 5–7, you'll find we're told exactly eight times that Jesus Christ is a priest *after the order of Melchizedek*.

Among the implications of this: the high priestly ministry of Jesus the Messiah was not limited to the Jewish people. Melchizedek was a

Gentile, unrelated to Abraham and his seed. Our great High Priest belongs to you and me and to all the world—Jews and Gentiles alike. He represents us before the Father, bestows blessings on us from the Father, and intercedes for us continually. He is a High Priest Forever according to the order of Melchizedek.

───※───

Jesus! my Shepherd, Husband, Friend,
O Prophet, Priest and King,
My Lord, my Life, my Way, my End,
Accept the praise I bring.

—JOHN NEWTON, 1779

THE MEDIATOR

There is one God and one Mediator between God and men,
the Man Christ Jesus.

— 1 TIMOTHY 2:5

MEDIATOR IS A WORD FREQUENTLY APPEARING IN OUR HEAD-
lines: "Union Asks for Mediator," "Mediator Joins Talks," "Parties
Call for Federal Mediator," "Mediator Breaks Impasse." Simply put,
a mediator serves as an intermediary between opposing parties with a
view toward reconciling the differences that divide them.

The ultimate mediation is between a fallen humanity and a holy
Creator. The patriarch Job expressed this in personal terms, saying,

> *For He is not a man, as I am,*
> *That I may answer Him,*
> *And that we should go to court together.*
> *Nor is there any mediator between us,*
> *Who may lay his hand on us both. (9:32–33)*

But there *is* a Mediator—the man Christ Jesus. This is a part of
His priestly ministry. The book of Hebrews says,

> *But now He has obtained a more excellent ministry, inasmuch as*
> *He is also Mediator of a better covenant, which was established on*
> *better promises. (8:6)*
> *He is the Mediator of the new covenant. (9:15)*

There is a high and holy God, far beyond the idle inklings of our
greatest comprehensions. He surpasses the bounds of both heaven
and earth, of both time and eternity. There is also a deep stain of in-
delible malevolence blighting our lives and pulling us into the abyss
of despair and toward the steaming fissures of hell.

Our Mediator suspended Himself between sky and soil, grasping
the balustrades of heaven with one hand and our sinking souls with

the other. With omnipotent energy, He pulled us upward. With omnipotent love, He pulled downward the infinite grace of the thrice-holy God.

As *The Message* puts it: "There's one God and only one, and one Priest-Mediator between God and us—Jesus, who offered Himself in exchange for everyone held captive by sin, to set them all free" (1 Tim. 2:5–6).

Have you accepted His terms of mediation? Have you thanked Him today for involving Himself in your personal labor-management dispute with the Almighty? What a Mediator is He!

Help us, Lord Jesus Christ, for we
A Mediator have in Thee.
Our works cannot salvation gain;
They merit but endless pain.
Have mercy, Lord!

—MARTIN LUTHER, 1524

THE REDEEMER

I know that my Redeemer lives,
And He shall stand at last on the earth;
And after my skin is destroyed, this I know,
That in my flesh I shall see God.

—Job 19:25–26

THE WAR IN IRAQ INCLUDED IMAGES THAT MADE US SHUD-
der: the kidnapping, torture, and beheading of innocent victims by
barbarous terrorists. Can you imagine being seized, unable to know
the outcome, expecting any moment to be decapitated? Can you envision the relief of rescue?

In a sense, we should feel the relief of rescue every day, for we have
a Redeemer who bought us back. The Son of Man gave His life as "a
ransom for many" (Matt. 20:28).

The term *redeem* comes from two words: *re* meaning "again," and
deem meaning "to buy." To buy back. To recover. The word gradually
came to refer to the purchasing of slaves or hostages for the purpose of
liberating them.

In biblical terms, redemption is the act by which God delivers us
from the bondage of sin by the sacrifice of Jesus Christ. Paul wrote,
"Christ has redeemed us from the curse of the law, having become a
curse for us" (Gal. 3:13). Peter reminds us we were not redeemed with
silver or gold, "but with the precious blood of Christ" (1 Pet. 1:19).
John recorded the song of the saints in Revelation 5:9: "You are worthy . . . / . . . for You were slain, / And have redeemed us to God by
Your blood."

It's this verse in Job, however, that most intrigues me; for he wrote
it long before Peter, Paul, or John articulated the doctrine of redemption. Some scholars think Job was the first book of the Bible to be
written, yet here it is: a fully developed statement of redemption, resurrection, and the return of Christ to earth.

Job tells us: (1) I have a Redeemer; (2) He is alive; (3) He will stand on earth at the end of history; (4) I will see Him with my eyes; (5) I may die, but that's not the end of me; (6) my body will be so thoroughly resurrected that even if my flesh decays, yet I shall be physically raised to see my Redeemer.

If Job, in the midst of all his problems and pain, could express such confidence, should we not also?

I know that my Redeemer liveth,
And on the earth again shall stand;
I know eternal life He giveth,
That grace and power are in His hand.

—JESSIE B. POUNDS, 1893

THE TESTATOR

For where there is a testament, there must also of
necessity be the death of a testator.

—Hebrews 9:16

A TESTATOR IS ONE WHO DIES LEAVING A LAST WILL AND TES-
tament in force. Years ago, my wife and I had a lawyer draw up a will
for us, not because we had much of this world's goods, but because
we had small children. We wanted to provide instructions for their
care should something happen to the both of us. Now our children
are grown and, thankfully, the will was never enacted.

The odd thing about a will is that it is utterly worthless as long as
its owner lives—none of its provisions are in effect and its instructions sit on the page perfectly useless. But the moment a person dies, it
becomes a powerful, living document with great authority and long-
lasting consequences.

Hebrews 9 says about Christ: "For where there is a testament,
there must also of necessity be the death of the testator." The New International Version is a little clearer: "In the case of a will, it is necessary to prove the death of the one who made it, because a will is in
force only when somebody has died; it never takes effect while the
one who made it is living" (vv. 16–17). The words *testament* and *will*
are synonyms in this passage.

The Old Testament—the Old Will—was put into effect by the
death of bulls and goats and sacrificial lambs. The New Testament—
the New Will—was put into effect by the death of Christ. So the title
Testator means that Christ made His wishes known, left all He had to
us, made us heirs of His glorious kingdom, and then died to put His
wishes into effect.

If you received a visit from an attorney today telling you of a large
and unexpected inheritance, wouldn't you be excited? The apostle
Paul has taught us to pray that the eyes of our understanding might

be opened that we might know the richness of our inheritance (Eph. 1:18). It is "an eternal inheritance" (Heb. 9:15), "an inheritance incorruptible and undefiled that does not fade way, reserved in heaven for you" (1 Pet. 1:4).

Heir of salvation, purchase of God,
Born of His Spirit, washed in His blood.

—FANNY CROSBY, 1873

THE BURNT OFFERING

*If his offering is a burnt sacrifice of the herd, let him offer a male
without blemish. . . . The burnt offering . . . will be accepted on his
behalf to make atonement for him.*

—LEVITICUS 1:3-4

THE FIRST TWO BOOKS OF THE BIBLE, GENESIS AND EXODUS,
brim with great stories and clearly illustrated lessons. But the next
book, Leviticus—well, that's another story. Most people find it dull
and somnolent.

I've come to appreciate Leviticus, though, because few books of the
Bible give us more information about Jesus Christ. It just has to be
discovered. As Dr. J. Sidlow Baxter once quipped, Leviticus wasn't
meant to be read, but to be studied.

For example, the first seven chapters of Leviticus describe the five
great offerings or sacrifices that God prescribed for the tabernacle
altar. Each of the five point prophetically toward the offering of the
Lamb of God on Calvary's cross. By studying the five Levitical sacrifices, we can learn five vital aspects of our Lord's redeeming death.

The first offering, described in Leviticus 1, is the burnt offering.
The distinguishing aspect of this sacrifice is given in Leviticus 1:9:
"The priest shall burn all on the altar." All on the altar. Nothing was
to remain. Nothing was to be eaten as food. The slain animal was totally consumed in the flames.

The sacrifice represented the totality of our Lord's offering of
Himself. He laid all on the altar for you and me. If the altar represents
the cross and the fire beneath it represents the judicial wrath of God,
then the Lord Jesus was a willing sacrifice who gave His last ounce of
strength for you and me. In Hebrews 10:6–7, Jesus said,

*In burnt offerings and sacrifices for sin
You had no pleasure.*

Then I said, "Behold, I have come—
In the volume of the book it is written of Me—
To do Your will, O God."

Romans 12 tells us that since our Burnt Sacrifice gave Himself fully for us, our logical act of worship is to offer ourselves as living sacrifices for Him. Have you placed "all on the altar"? Are you holding anything back from the one who became a Burnt Offering for you?

Is your all on the altar of sacrifice laid?
Your heart does the Spirit control?
You can only be blest,
And have peace and sweet rest,
As you yield Him your body and soul.

—Elisha A. Hoffman, 1900

HE GRAIN OFFERING

When anyone offers a grain offering to the LORD, his offering shall be of fine flour. And he shall pour oil on it, and put frankincense on it.

—LEVITICUS 2:1

DO YOU EVER CHANGE YOUR MIND? NONE OF US IS PERFECT, and as we grow and learn more, our opinions often change and evolve. As we gain new information, we reach new and perhaps more correct conclusions. William Blake once said, "The man who never alters his opinion is like standing water and breeds reptiles of the mind."

One man, however, never changed His mind about anything. He never suffered from insufficient knowledge, and He never harbored a wrong opinion. He was utterly faultless in every thought that wound through His brain. He was perfectly correct in every position on which He stood. He was the sinless Son of God.

That's the significance of the grain offering, for it was to be an offering of the *finest* flour.

The first seven chapters of Leviticus describe the five great offerings God prescribed for the tabernacle altar. Each one points to Christ, thereby giving us a pentagon of truths about Calvary. The first sacrifice, the burnt offering of Leviticus 1, was totally consumed by the flames, representing the totality of our Lord's sacrifice on the cross for us.

The second offering, described in Leviticus 2, involved no shedding of blood, hence it spoke more of our Lord's life than of His death. It was a grain offering. The Israelites were to bring grain or bread to the tabernacle as an offering to the Lord. This not only provided food for the priests, but it demonstrated another aspect of our Lord's sacrifice—our Lord's flawless humanity. Jesus was the Bread of Life, made of fine flour. The phrase "fine flour" occurs five times in

Leviticus 2 and points toward our Lord's sinless, upright, holy, perfect life.

He is altogether holy, and our lives are filled with holiness and wisdom only as they conform to His. Jesus is the ultimate role model for our lives, and we should match our behavior to His. His very life is as pure as premium flour, and we're nourished as we draw strength from Him. Just as a hungry man is satisfied by a hot loaf of home-baked bread, our lives are satisfied with Him who gave Himself as our grain offering, our Bread of Life, our Savior, who was crushed by the mortar and pestle of Calvary.

Of all wonders that can thrill thee,
And with adoration fill thee,
What than this can greater be,
That Himself to thee He giveth?
He that eateth ever liveth,
For the Bread of Life is He.

—THOMAS AQUINAS, C. 1260

THE PEACE OFFERING

When his offering is a sacrifice of a peace offering.

—LEVITICUS 3:1

THE THIRD OLD TESTAMENT SACRIFICE WAS THE PEACE OF-
fering, described in Leviticus 3. If the burnt offering represented the
totality of our Lord's sacrifice and the grain offering represented His
quality of His humanity, the peace offering represented the tranquility His sacrifice brings to our lives.

In the peace offering, the animal was to be killed, its blood sprinkled on the altar, its fat burned on the grate, and its meat was to be
eaten and enjoyed by the worshiper. According to Leviticus 17, every
time an Israelite slaughtered an animal for food, he was to consider it
a peace offering. It was celebratory.

In short, our lives should be a celebration of inner peace, for "He
Himself is our peace" (Eph. 2:14). He purchased peace for us on the
cross, and He gives us peace freely: "Having been justified by grace
through faith, we have peace with God" through Him who said,
"Peace I leave with you, My peace I give to you" (Rom. 5:1; John
14:27). The Bible promises, "Great peace have those who love Your
law, and nothing causes them to stumble" (Psalm 119:165).

Just last week, I had a hard jolt in the form of bad news on the tele-
phone. For a few minutes, I was downcast as I absorbed the message.
Then I recalled the promise of Isaiah 55:12: "You shall go out with
joy, and be led out with peace." If Christ died so that I can go out into
each day with peace, why should I remain gloomy?

Later the "bad news" sparked a chain reaction that resulted in a
number of good things happening. I realized afresh the importance of
walking by faith and choosing to go out with peace. The old Puritan
Thomas Watson put it this way: "Christ not only prayed for peace,
but bled for peace. Christ suffered on the cross that He might cement

Christians together with His blood; as He prayed for peace, so He paid for peace."[16]

He is our Peace, our Prince of Peace, our Source of Peace, and our Peace Offering. During His earthly life, He lived in great depths of personal peace, and when He returned to Heaven, He left His peace behind for you and me. "Peace I leave with you," He said.

Today, go out with joy and be led out with peace!

I saw the cross of Jesus, when burdened with my sin;
I sought the cross of Jesus, to give me peace within;
I brought my soul to Jesus, He cleansed it in His blood;
And in the cross of Jesus I found my peace with God.

—FREDERICK WHITFIELD, 1829–1904

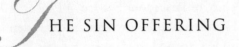

The Sin Offering

*Let him offer to the LORD for his sin which he has sinned
a young bull without blemish as a sin offering.*

—LEVITICUS 4:3

"TO LIVE WITHOUT FORGIVENESS IS A MISERABLE THING."
A woman in prison spoke those words. She had been convicted of
starting a forest fire that destroyed 140,000 acres and consumed 132
homes in Colorado. She was appealing to the public to pardon her for
her terrible mistake.

When we say or do something damaging to others, it brings guilt
and shame upon us, reducing our self-esteem and sense of worth.
Even worse, sin, when it is finished, brings death. To live without forgiveness is miserable indeed.

In Leviticus 4, the Lord provided an answer to sin's ravages. He instructed any Israelite who sinned to bring an innocent animal to the
tabernacle altar as a sacrifice. The sinner laid his hand on the head of
the animal, then slaughtered it. This was called the sin offering, and it
conveyed the idea of transference. God created a method of dealing
with sin that allowed the sinner to transfer his guilt onto the head of
an innocent victim who would then die in his or her stead.

We now know that the blood of the animal had no power in itself.
It was symbolic, pointing to Christ. Isaiah 53 says:

> *Surely He has borne our griefs*
> *And carried our sorrows. . . .*
> *He was wounded for our transgressions,*
> *He was bruised for our iniquities;*
> *The chastisement for our peace was upon Him,*
> *And by His stripes we are healed.*
> *All we like sheep have gone astray;*

We have turned, every one, to his own way;
And the LORD *has laid on Him the iniquity of us all. (vv. 4–6)*

Christ Himself bore the penalty for our sins on the cross, that we might be abundantly pardoned—just as though we had never sinned at all.

Think of the thing about which you feel worst. If you could go back and change it, you would, but that's impossible. What, then, can you do with your guilt and shame? You can push it down deeper into your own heart where it will eventually poison your personality. You can push it onto others, blaming them for your problems. Or you can push your sins onto Christ, who bears our transgressions.

Christ has for sin atonement made
What a wonderful Savior!
We are redeemed, the price is paid
What a wonderful Savior!

—ELISHA A. HOFFMAN, 1891

THE TRESPASS OFFERING

He shall bring his trespass offering to the LORD for his sin which he has committed.

—LEVITICUS 5:6

THE BOOK OF EXODUS ENDS WITH A DESCRIPTION OF THE ancient tabernacle, and the book of Leviticus opens with a description of the five sacrifices Israel was to offer on the great bronze altar near the entrance to the tabernacle courtyard. Again, these five offerings give us five aspects of the life and death of Jesus Christ, our great sacrifice for sin.

─• *Jesus is our Burnt Offering: He offered Himself in totality.*

─• *He is our Grain Offering: He offered His perfect humanity.*

─• *He is our Peace Offering: He offered Himself for our tranquility.*

─• *He is our Sin Offering: He offered Himself to bear our penalty.*

─• *And He is our Trespass Offering: He offered Himself as sin's remedy.*

The trespass offering was very similar to the sin offering, except that it seemed to deal with both the sin and the damage sin had done to the sinner and to others. Leviticus 5:16, for example, says, "And he [the sinner] shall make restitution for the harm that he has done."

Behold the greatness of Christ's redemption. He not only forgives our sin, but He heals the damage sin has caused to our own lives. Even better, He can help and heal others whom we have hurt by our sins.

Have your words and deeds hurt someone? You've apologized. You've asked forgiveness; but you can't repair the damage. Entrust it to the Lord. As we wait upon Him, He can weave the darkened strands of sin into a beautiful tapestry, using it all for good in the final analysis. We have to trust Him with that, because to repair sin's damage is often beyond our ability.

Jesus, however, faces no impossible situations. He can do anything. He is our Burnt Offering, our Grain Offering, our Peace Offering, our Sin Offering, and our Trespass Offering. He totally gave His perfect humanity to bear sin's penalty, to provide sin's remedy, and to bring us tranquility. That, in a nutshell, is Leviticus 1–5. And that, in summation, is the precious work of Christ, the Lamb of God.

How blest is he whose trespass
Hath freely been forgiv'n,
Whose sin is wholly covered
Before the sight of Heav'n.

— 1912 PSALTER

$\mathcal{T}$HE BIRD THAT WAS KILLED

[The priest shall] dip . . . the living bird in the blood of
the bird that was killed over the running water.
And he shall sprinkle it seven times on him who is to be cleansed
from the leprosy, and shall pronounce him clean,
and shall let the living bird loose in the open field.

—LEVITICUS 14:6–7

THE BOOK OF LEVITICUS, WRITTEN CENTURIES BEFORE Christ, is full of pictures foreshadowing our Lord in His roles as sacrifice and High Priest. The unusual picture given in this verse involves those who have been healed from leprosy.

Picture a man who had contracted leprosy. He's condemned. He's diseased, his skin aflame with repugnant running sores. He's been forced to abandon home and hearth. His wife, children, and grandchildren no longer associate with him, for to do so would risk infection. The poor wretch has been driven outside the camp, quarantined and isolated, sick and suffering.

He is a picture of you or me in our sins. This is symbolic of a poor sinner, lost and sick and diseased of soul, for the Bible likens leprosy to sin. What leprosy is to the body, sin is to the soul: a disfiguring and deadly disease that ruins our lives and makes us outcasts from God and from hope.

But there is healing. And in Leviticus 14, we're told that when the healing occurred in Old Testament times, a little ceremony took place. The priest brought out two birds. One was killed in a clay pot over running water, and the other bird was dipped in the bloody water and set free to fly into the heavens and to make his home in the thin fresh air.

It's a beautiful picture of you and me. Though we were diseased sinners, Jesus Christ died for us and we are washed in His blood. Our souls are thus set free to soar in life, to "mount up with wings like eagles," and to make our home in the heavens (Isa. 40:31).

Are you sprinkled in the blood of the Bird that was slain? Are you mounting upward on the wings of grace?

Come in poverty and meanness,
Come defiled, without, within;
From infection and uncleanness,
From the leprosy of sin,
Wash your robes and make them white;
Ye shall walk with God in light.

—JAMES MONTGOMERY, 1819

MAN OF SORROWS

He is despised and rejected by men,
A Man of sorrows and acquainted with grief.

—ISAIAH 53:3

THE WORD *SORROW* COMES FROM AN OLD SLAVONIC WORD meaning *sickness*. Our English word implies deep distress and regret, usually over the loss of something dearly loved. All of us know this plunging, purging grief and sadness, and some people seem to live with it perpetually.

Jesus understands perfectly. The word *sorrow* occurs 108 times from Genesis to Revelation, and Isaiah described Jesus as a Man of Sorrows. How could it be otherwise when He came to bear our sins and to die for lost, unappreciative humanity? He gave His sorrow full vent in the Garden of Gethsemane in Matthew 26:37–38: "He began to be sorrowful and deeply distressed. Then He said to them, 'My soul is exceedingly sorrowful, even to death.'"

Christ assumed our sorrows that we might experience His joy, and He lifted our burdens that we might be heirs of hope.

Isaiah had predicted,

> *He is despised and rejected by men,*
> *A Man of sorrows and acquainted with grief.*
> *And we hid, as it were, our faces from Him;*
> *He was despised, and we did not esteem Him.*
> *Surely He has borne our griefs*
> *And carried our sorrows. . . .*
> *He was bruised for our iniquities . . .*
> *And by His stripes we are healed. (53:3–5)*

If you're downcast today, take heart. You're not always going to feel as badly as you do right now. The clouds will break, and the sun will shine again. No matter what it is, the burden will lift, and life will once again be fun and fulfilling. That's His promise. The world has temporary pleasures, but lasting and permanent sorrow, while the Christian endures moments of sorrow but has lasting and permanent joy.

Jesus said:

Your sorrow will be turned into joy. A woman, when she is in labor, has sorrow because her hour has come; but as soon as she has given birth to the child, she no longer remembers the anguish, for joy that a human being has been born into the world. Therefore you now have sorrow; but I will see you again and your heart will rejoice, and your joy no one will take from you. (John 16:20–22)

Man of Sorrows! what a name
For the Son of God, Who came
Ruined sinners to reclaim.
Hallelujah! What a Savior!

—PHILIP P. BLISS, 1875

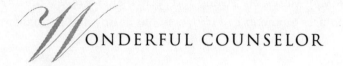

WONDERFUL COUNSELOR

For to us a child is born,
to us a Son is given;
and the government will be on his shoulders.
And he will be called Wonderful Counselor.

—ISAIAH 9:6 (NIV)[17]

COUNSELING IS BIG BUSINESS. YOU MAY HAVE A LEGAL COUN-selor. Perhaps a financial counselor. Maybe a marriage counselor. Many people seek vocational counseling. Every school has guidance counselors. Our world is complicated, and we need wisdom beyond ourselves in dealing with vexing issues.

But only one Counselor is always available, utterly unfailing, and entirely affordable. The triune God has His shingle out: God the Father, God the Son, God the Spirit. His counseling practice is open for business.

GOD THE FATHER

You will guide me with Your counsel,

> *And afterward receive me to glory. (Psalm 73:24)*

The LORD of hosts

> *. . . Is wonderful in counsel and excellent in guidance.*
> *(Isaiah 28:29)*

GOD THE SON

And His name will be called

> *Wonderful, Counselor. (Isaiah 9:6)*

I will ask the Father, and He will give you another Counselor to be with you. (John 14:16 NIV). (By referring to the Holy Spirit as *"another* Counselor," Jesus was claiming that role for Himself as well.)

GOD THE HOLY SPIRIT

—⟡ *The Counselor, the Holy Spirit, whom the Father will send in my name, will teach you all things and will remind you of everything I have said to you. (John 14:26 NIV)*

How does Christ counsel us today? Primarily through His Word. By prayerfully reading His Word, we discern His voice, His reassurance, His correction, His training, His wisdom, and His direction in life. "Your testimonies are also my delight," says Psalm 119:24, "and my counselors."

If my day starts without a quiet period of reflection and prayer, I feel that I'm clueless all day. If, during times of distress, I don't search out a promise to sustain me, I feel like falling apart. How wonderful to have a personal Counselor twenty-four hours a day, always available, offering infinite wisdom! How wonderful our Wonderful Counselor!

Every day, the Lord Himself is near me
With a special mercy for each hour;
All my cares He fain would bear, and cheer me,
He Whose Name is Counselor and Power.

—KAROLINA SANDELL-BERG, 1865

EVERLASTING FATHER

And His name will be called
Wonderful, Counselor, Mighty God,
Everlasting Father.

—Isaiah 9:6

In what sense can we call Jesus the Everlasting Father? At first glance, this puzzles us, for the Messiah is distinguished within the Trinity from God the Father. How can the Son be the Father?

Some commentators insist that the best rendering of these words from the original Hebrew is "Father of Everlasting" or "Father of Eternity." Among the Jews, the word *father* conveyed the idea of originator or source, suggesting that Jesus is creator of both time and eternity; or more accurately, He is our source and provider for everlasting life.

Others suggest that the word *Father* should not be interpreted in a trinitarian sense, but in the sense of protector and provider. Isaiah 22:21, for example, says about a man named Eliakim, "He shall be a father to the inhabitants of Jerusalem." In other words, he would protect the city. Ancient Near Eastern kings often used such language of themselves. For example, Azitawadda of Adana (c. 800 BC) declared that Baal had made him "a father and a mother" to his people.[18]

Still others suggest that this title is forever shrouded in the unfathomable imponderables of the Trinity. Jesus Himself once said, "I and My Father are one" (John 10:30). Hebrews 1:3 declares that Christ was "the brightness of [the Father's] glory and the express image of His person." The apostle Paul said, "For in Him dwells all the fullness of the Godhead bodily" (Col. 2:9).

One final theory is that Christ is our Everlasting Father in this sense: He is our spiritual parent; He bestows our new birth. Charles H. Spurgeon held this view; Warren Wiersbe agrees. He wrote,

"Christ is called the 'Everlasting Father' and this is the reason why: His death and travail on the cross have made possible God's family of saved sinners."[19]

Which theory is correct? All of them contain logic and truth, and so I am uncertain of which meaning Isaiah had in mind. It is comforting, however, to visualize the "fathering" graces of Jesus Christ. Spurgeon put as a prayer in his *Morning and Evening*: "O Lord Jesus, the Everlasting Father, You are my spiritual Parent; unless Your Spirit had breathed into me the breath of a new, holy, and spiritual life, I would have been to this day 'dead in trespasses and sins.' My heavenly life is wholly derived from You, to You I ascribe it. My life is hid with Christ in God."[20]

O God, we praise Thee, and confess
That Thou the only Lord
And everlasting Father art,
By all the earth adored.

—NICHOLAS BRADY AND NAHUM TATE, 1703

A TENDER PLANT

Who has believed our report?
And to whom has the arm of the LORD been revealed?
For He shall grow up before Him as a tender plant.

—ISAIAH 53:1–2

THOUGH WRITTEN SEVEN HUNDRED YEARS BEFORE THE birth of Christ, this passage (Isaiah 52:13–53:12) brims over with specific predictions regarding the rejection, crucifixion, and resurrection of Jesus Christ.

The phrase "tender plant" gives us an indication of His descent from the house and lineage of David. Often in the Old Testament, the Davidic/messianic line is symbolized as a plant. Isaiah had used this figure of speech previously: "A shoot will come up from the stump of Jesse [the father of David]; / from his roots a Branch will bear fruit. / The Spirit of the LORD will rest on Him" (11:1–2 NIV). It's an immense thought. Though the line and lineage of David appeared to be decayed and dead, yet a little sap still lived in the dry roots, and a little sapling sprang out of it, a lad in Nazareth who grew up before the Lord as a Tender Plant from the stump of Jesse.

Several times the Bible likens us, too, to trees. Psalm 1, for example, promises success and prosperity to those who persistently meditate on God's Word. They will be like trees "planted by the rivers of water" (v. 3). Psalm 92 says, "Those who are planted in the house of the LORD / Shall flourish in the courts of our God. / They shall still bear fruit in old age; / They shall be fresh and flourishing" (vv. 13–14).

Jeremiah 17:7–8 puts it in vivid terms:

> *Blessed is the man who trusts in the LORD,*
> *And whose hope is the LORD.*
> *For he shall be like a tree planted by waters,*
> *Which spreads out its roots by the river,*

And will not fear when heat comes;
But its leaf will be green,
And will not be anxious in the year of drought,
Nor will cease from yielding fruit.

Are you well rooted in Christ?

❧

Not by the will of man, or mortal seed,
But by the Spirit's breathed mysterious grace
The Word of God became our flesh indeed,
And grew a tender plant of human race.

— AMBROSE, FOURTH CENTURY

MY STRENGTH AND MY SONG

The LORD, the LORD, is my strength and my song;
and He has become my salvation.
With joy you will draw water
from the wells of salvation.

—ISAIAH 12:2–3 (NIV)

THE BRITISH PREACHER DR. MARTYN LLOYD-JONES ONCE wrote, "Unhappy Christians are, to say the least, a poor recommendation for the Christian Faith. . . . In a sense a depressed Christian is a contradiction in terms."[21]

It isn't possible to be happy all the time, and even Jesus Himself wept. The writers of the Psalms suffered many distresses, and the patriarch Job was cast down for a spell. But there's never a time when we should lose the joy of the Lord or find ourselves unable to exalt in our God.

After all, the word *rejoice* occurs 287 times in the Bible, and the corresponding word *joy* occurs another 181 times. The shortest verse in the English Bible is "Jesus wept" (John 11:35), but the shortest verse in the original Greek is 1 Thessalonians 5:16: "Rejoice always." The apostle Paul noted this apparent contradiction when he described himself as "sorrowful, yet always rejoicing" (2 Cor. 6:10).

In short, the Lord is our Strength, our Song, and our salvation—and we're to draw living water from the well of salvation with joy.

Henry Baker did just that. The son of a British vice admiral of the Navy, Henry became an Anglican clergyman and a nineteenth-century hymnist whose greatest work, *Hymns Ancient and Modern,* sold sixty million copies and set the world singing. My favorite Baker hymn is "The King of Love My Shepherd Is," based on Psalm 23. But another of his greatest works is "Rejoice Today with One Accord." Take a moment and sing this to yourself. It fits the majestic strains of "A Mighty Fortress."

Rejoice today with one accord,
Sing out with exultation;
Rejoice and praise our mighty Lord,
Whose arm hath brought salvation;
His works of love proclaim
The greatness of His Name;
For He is God alone
Who hath His mercy shown;
Let all His saints adore Him!

—Henry Baker, 1861

MY ELECT ONE

Behold! My Servant whom I uphold,
My Elect One in whom My soul delights!
I have put My Spirit upon Him;
He will bring forth justice to the Gentiles.

—ISAIAH 42:1

AS I WRITE THESE WORDS, I'M HOLED AWAY IN A SECLUDED spot, looking out my window through orange-tinged leaves to a gentle lake. I had to get away, to think through things, to pray, to tranquilize my soul. I didn't tell my staff, and no one but my wife knows where I am. I've turned off my cell phone, and I'm just AWOL.

This is the passage the Lord has used today to speak to me, and if I had a dozen pages, I could wax eloquent about it. Seeing I don't have that much space, I can sum it up this way: the secret of unburdening the soul lies with the Lord Jesus, God's Elect One.

In Matthew 12, this passage is quoted as applying to Jesus, and it seems to presage His baptism. In Isaiah's original wording, we read that the Holy Spirit would rest upon the Servant in whom God delights. As worded in Matthew 12, the Holy Spirit is said to rest on "My Servant . . . / . . . In whom My soul is well pleased" (v. 18).

We think immediately of Jesus at the River Jordan, dripping with the waters of baptism, the Holy Spirit descending on Him in the shape of a dove. He hears the thunderous voice of the Father saying, "This is My beloved Son, in whom I am well pleased" (Matt. 3:17).

Here's the point for me: if God the Father so delights in His Son in whom He is so pleased, shouldn't Jesus be the one great delight of my life too? Shouldn't I be thrilled with His abiding presence? Shouldn't I be perennially renewed by His fellowship? Shouldn't I be eager every day to introduce Him to others and to speak of Him to my friends and acquaintances?

The Bible says, "Delight yourself also in the LORD, / And He shall give you the desires of your heart" (Ps. 37:4).

Jesus Christ is God's Elect One. His Chosen One. His Anointed One. His Special Servant in whom He delights and with whom He is well pleased. As the hymnist said, "Who can cheer the heart like Jesus by His presence all divine; / True and tender, pure and precious, O how blest to call Him mine!"

All that thrills my soul is Jesus,
He is more than life to me.
And the fairest of ten thousand,
In my blessed Lord I see.

—THORO HARRIS, 1931

A POLISHED SHAFT

In the shadow of His hand He has hidden Me,
And made Me a polished shaft;
In His quiver He has hidden me.

—ISAIAH 49:2

THIS IS ONE OF THE BIBLE'S MOST UNFAMILIAR AND UN-
usual depictions of Christ. God the Father is pictured here as a great
Archer, and in highest heaven He picks up the divine bow and shoots
His Son to earth like an arrow.

But did the Polished Shaft miss its mark? At one point, according
to this chapter, the Messiah was tempted to wonder whether His efforts were in vain. He was, after all, tempted in all points as we are.

Do you ever feel that way? If you're a parent, preacher, missionary,
Bible-study leader, Sunday-school teacher, soul-winner, or caregiver,
you surely encounter times of discouragement. As you seek to share
your faith with others, you may sometimes wonder if your efforts are
wasted.

But the Father reassured the Son in Isaiah 49, saying, in effect:
"Not only will You redeem My chosen people, the Jews, but that will
prove too small a task. You will bring salvation to the whole earth and
the message of hope to Jews and Gentiles alike."

We see this clearly as we read the entire passage in the New Living
Translation:

> *The LORD called me before my birth. . . . He made my words of*
> *judgment as sharp as a sword. He has hidden me in the shadow of his*
> *hand. I am like a sharp arrow in his quiver. . . .*
>
> *I replied, "But my work all seems so useless! I have spent my*
> *strength for nothing and to no purpose at all. Yet I leave it all in the*
> *LORD's hand; I will trust God for my reward."*
>
> *And now the LORD speaks—he who formed me in my mother's*

womb to be his servant, who commissioned me to bring his people of Israel back to him. The LORD has honored me, and my God has given me strength. He says, "You will do more than restore the people of Israel to me. I will make you a light to the Gentiles, and you will bring my salvation to the ends of the earth." (Isaiah 49:1–2, 4–6 NLT)

There are no insignificant acts for those in God's will. Trust Him and be faithful.

> *Sometimes I feel discouraged,*
> *And think my work's in vain,*
> *But then the Holy Spirit*
> *Revives my soul again.*

—BLACK AMERICAN SPIRITUAL, NINETEENTH CENTURY

A SANCTUARY

He will be as a sanctuary.

—ISAIAH 8:14

I'VE HAD A LITTLE LIFELONG PROBLEM WITH MY NERVES. Not that I'm particularly unstable or prone to breakdowns; it's just that in moments of urgency, crisis, or extremity, I tend to panic and hyperventilate. Sometimes the results are hilarious.

Once, for example, our smoke detectors went off and I thought the house was on fire. Having previously escaped a burning building, I had flashbacks and flew into sheer panic. Running to the phone, I dialed 411 instead of 911, then became confused when the operator asked me what number I wanted. "What's the number for 911?" I screamed at her. Not waiting for an answer, I threw down the phone and began running around like a madman, heart pounding, trying to get everyone out of the house. As it turned out, there was no fire at all and I felt like an idiot.

Other times, it's not so comical, and many times I've reacted to terrible news by caving in to fear instead of exercising faith. But I've learned through the years that His Word is more powerful than my worries, and His promises are greater than my moments of panic.

Isaiah 8:14 is a clear reference to Christ, and Jesus is called our Sanctuary. The Hebrew word *miqdash* refers to a holy place, a temple, a place of sanctity and safety. I like the way the Amplified Bible puts it: "He shall be a sanctuary [a sacred and indestructible asylum to those who reverently fear and trust in Him]."

I'd like to give you two words that may help if you're panic-prone. They are FOMBAS and TILIS. Proverbs 29:25 says, "The fear of man brings a snare, / But whoever trusts in the LORD shall be safe." There are two ways to live: FOMBAS (Fear Of Man Brings A Snare), or TILIS (Trusting In The Lord Is Safe).

Our lives are "hidden with Christ in God," and "God has not given us a spirit of fear," but the Spirit of power, love, and clear thinking (Col. 3:3; 2 Tim. 1:7). For me the change from fear to faith has been gradual and progressive, but undeniable. It's a gift of grace and a process of growth. It helps when I think of Christ as a Sanctuary, a Rock of safety, a high tower, a Hen who gathers her chicks under her wings, or one of the Bible's other manifold pictures of security in the Savior.

Should storms of sevenfold vengeance roll,
And shake this earth from pole to pole;
No flaming bolt could daunt my face,
For Jesus is my hiding place.

—JEHOIDA BREWER, 1776

A SHELTER FROM THE TEMPEST

A man will be as a hiding place from the wind,
And a cover from the tempest,
As rivers of water in a dry place,
As the shadow of a great rock in a weary land.

—Isaiah 32:2

About whom was Isaiah writing? Isaiah 32:1 says, "Behold, a king will reign in righteousness, / And princes will rule with justice." Then comes verse 2 with its fourfold picture of safety and security:

1. A hiding place from the wind.

2. A cover from the tempest.

3. Rivers of water in a dry place.

4. The shadow of a great rock in a weary land.

I think it's speaking of the protective, comforting presence of the King who reigns in righteousness. The New Living Translation says: "Look, a righteous king is coming! And honest princes will rule under him. He will shelter Israel from the storm and the wind. He will refresh her as a river in the desert and as the cool shadow of a large rock in a hot and weary land."

I know it's true for me. In moments of great anger or anxiety, I've fled to the Lord, burrowing myself away in my journal, in the Scriptures, and in prayer. I've turned things over to the Lord, knowing that I hadn't the power to make them right. I've found that "the name of the LORD is a strong tower" in which to find safety (Prov. 18:10). I've strengthened myself with Paul's words that we have died, and our lives are hidden in Christ (Col. 3:3).

When I was a child, we sang an old hymn in our church entitled, "Master, the Tempest Is Raging." One line has stayed with me: "No storm can swallow the ship where lies / The Master of ocean and earth and skies."

On an evening some time ago, when a windstorm of worry blew through my heart, I questioned God's seeming reluctance to answer my prayers. I'd been intensely praying about a difficult matter for some years, but no answer seemed forthcoming. In fact, all seemed worse. So I determined to treat it as a shelter. His care is waterproof. Taking up my pen, I wrote another prayer—a different one.

*Lord, answer in Your own good time
And in your own best way.
I wait on you in childlike faith
And in this storm I'll say:
You still the wind, you calm the heart,
You know my every fear.
I'll pray and trust and wait on You,
And find a shelter here.*

$\mathcal{M}$Y RIGHTEOUS SERVANT

By His knowledge My righteous Servant shall justify many,
for He shall bear their iniquities.

—ISAIAH 53:11

JOHN MARRANT (1755–1791), A YOUNG BLACK MUSICIAN IN Charleston, South Carolina, was converted when he passed a church one night while returning from a party. "A crazy man was hallooing there," he recalled. A chum dared him to enter the church and blow his French horn during the sermon. Elbowing his way into the church, Marrant was about to blast his horn when the preacher, evangelist George Whitefield, recited his text: "Prepare to meet thy God, O Israel" (Amos 4:12). This led to the young man's conversion.

Marrant was soon so zealous for the Lord that he launched into the Southern frontier to share the gospel with Native Americans—but it didn't go as planned. The Cherokees captured Marrant and condemned him to die the next morning. He spent his last night singing and praying aloud, much to the astonishment of his guard, who kept trying to figure out with whom he was speaking in the empty hut.

The next morning, Marrant was led out for execution. There he learned his captors planned to strip him naked, stretch him out, and pierce him with scores of sharp turpentine sticks that they would then set afire. After the stakes had burned down to his skin, the Cherokees would turn him over to receive the same treatment on his backside. Then they would throw him into a blazing fire to finish the job.

Hearing the news, Marrant burst into tears and began praying earnestly in the Cherokee tongue. So moved were his captors that they took him to the chief and later to the king of the Cherokees, where he sought to explain his faith. Opening his Bible, Marrant read Isaiah 53, about God's Righteous Servant who was "wounded for our transgressions, / . . . [and] bruised for our iniquities" (v. 5). Several Cherokees came under deep conviction, including the king and his daughter, who were converted. John Marrant spent the next two years in those parts, preaching and evangelizing, following in the footsteps of God's Righteous Servant.[22]

Following Jesus is a great adventure, and we should expect the unexpected. Jesus was God's Righteous Servant who justified many (Isa. 53:11), and we're to be Christ's righteous servants to tell many about it.

While Thou didst on earth appear,
Servant to Thy servants here,
Mindful of Thy place above,
All Thy life was prayer and love.

—CHARLES WESLEY, 1767

OD

In the beginning was the Word, and the Word was with God, and the Word was God.

—JOHN 1:1

"WHEN I AM TOLD THAT GOD BECAME MAN," SAID OLD MARtin Luther, "I can follow the idea, but I just do not understand what it means. For what man, if left to his natural promptings, if he were God, would humble himself to lie in the feedbox of a donkey or to hang upon a cross?"[23]

Luther captured the wonder that John expressed as he opened his Gospel by describing Jesus Christ—the Word!—as God Himself. The Gospels of Matthew and Luke describe the birth of Christ in lowly human terms, but John opens His Gospel with a different kind of nativity account: *The Word was God. . . . The Word became flesh and dwelled among us!*

In calling Jesus the *Word,* John used the Greek term *Logos,* which meant "message, communication, word, tangible expression of thought." This was John's special title for Jesus that he used in his Gospel, in his epistles, and in the book of Revelation. Jesus was the tangible expression of God for humanity.

From time to time, someone challenges me on whether the Bible really teaches that Jesus Christ is very God of very God. I reply that there's no question as to that teaching in Scripture. Evidence for the deity of Christ is found by following several different lines of observation in the New Testament, but the simplest way to demonstrate it is by re-reading some of our greatest verses on the subject, such as these opening verses of the Gospel of John.

Consider also the affirmation at the end of John's Gospel, when Thomas exclaims to the risen Christ, "My Lord and My God" (John 20:28).

In Isaiah 9:6, Jesus is called "the Mighty God." Hebrews 1:8 says of

His Johannine Names

Him, "Your throne, O God, is forever and ever." Romans 9:5 says, "From [the patriarchs] is traced the human ancestry of Christ, who is God over all, forever praised!" (NIV). The Bible says, "For in Him dwells all the fullness of the Godhead bodily" (Colossians 2:9). And in Titus 2:13, the apostle Paul tells us to be on the lookout for "that blessed hope and glorious appearing of our great God and Savior Jesus Christ."

This truth can never charge, erode, or evaporate; it's at the heart of our hopes and in the center of our certainty. It's the doctrine that puts the backbone in the Bible and that puts steel in the Christian's soul. Jesus is—always has been and always will be—God!

Jesus is God! O! could I now
But compass earth and sea,
To teach and tell the single truth,
How happy should I be!

—FREDERICK W. FABER, 1862

THE SAVIOR OF THE WORLD

We ourselves have heard Him and we know
that this is indeed the Christ, the Savior of the world.

—JOHN 4:42

THE GOSPELS USE THE TERM *SAVIOR* TO DESCRIBE JESUS ONLY twice. The first occasion is at His birth, when the angel proclaimed: "For there is born to you this day in the city of David a Savior, who is Christ the Lord" (Luke 2:11). The other occasion is in John 4:42, when the Samaritans called Jesus the "Savior of the world."

This term appears twice in the book of Acts as a reference to Christ. In making his defense before the ruling council, Peter said of Jesus: "Him God has exalted to His right hand to be Prince and Savior" (Acts 5:31). Paul, in one of his first recorded sermons, added, "God raised up for Israel a Savior—Jesus" (Acts 13:23). In their epistles, Paul used this term a dozen times and Peter, five times. It's a word that comes from a Greek verb meaning: "to save, to rescue."

I have a friend who's a lifeguard. Recently I asked if he'd saved many lives this summer, and he immediately told me the number of "saves" credited to him.

"It must be exciting," I said.

"Nothing's more exhilarating or terrifying or fulfilling than plunging into cold water, knowing someone's life depends on me," he told me. "Nothing makes my heart pound like that. It's the best feeling in the world, to burst through the waves with all my strength to pull people to safety, sometimes even against their will if they're panicking. I wish I could do it all the time."

"Sounds a lot like soul-winning," I quipped.

Pioneer missionary Willard Hotchkiss wrote:

I have dwelt forty years practically alone in Africa. I have been thirty-nine times stricken with the fever, three times attacked by lions, and several times by rhinoceri, but let me say to you, I would gladly go through the whole thing again, if I could have the joy of again bringing that word "Savior" and flashing it into the darkness that envelopes another tribe in Central Africa.[24]

Have you told someone recently of the Savior?

Lift up your heads, ye mighty gates;
Behold, the King of glory waits;
The King of kings is drawing near;
The Savior of the world is here!

—GEORG WEISSEL, 1642

THE LAMB OF GOD

The next day John saw Jesus coming toward him, and said,
"Behold! The Lamb of God who takes away the sin of the world!"

—JOHN 1:29

THERE WAS NEVER A ROUGHER PREACHER THAN JOHN, NOR A more sublime theme than the Lamb of God. When I picture the scene in my mind's eye, it's a jolting image. The rugged Baptist, dressed in frayed leather like a mountain man, eating grasshoppers and honey, wild glint in his eye, trashing around in the river, warning his generation of impending judgment. And then Jesus shows up from nowhere, and John's demeanor changes. His face softens and he begins talking about lambs. About a Lamb. The Lamb of God, he says, who takes away the sins of the world. He suddenly becomes an astute and learned theologian, for he reaches into the Hebrew Scriptures and discovers the master key that unlocks the meaning of all the sacrificial systems of Jewish tradition. Jesus is the fulfillment of them all — the Lamb of God who takes away the sins of the world.

Peter Cartwright, the backwoods Methodist evangelist who served as a circuit riding preacher for fifty-three years, from 1803 to 1856, was equally struck by John. Here is what he said about himself and John 1:29:

A Methodist preacher in those days, when he felt that God had called him to preach, instead of hunting up a college or Biblical institute, hunted up a hardy pony of a horse, and some traveling apparatus, and with his library always at hand, namely, Bible, Hymn Book, and Discipline, he started. . . . With a text that never wore out nor grew stale, he cried, "Behold the Lamb of God, that taketh away the sins of the world." In this way he went through storms of wind, hail, snow, and rain; climbed hills and mountains, traversed valleys, plunged through swamps. . . . Often he slept in dirty cabins, on earthen floors, before

---

His Johannine Names

the fire; ate roasting ears for bread, drank buttermilk for coffee, or sage tea for imperial; took, with a hearty zest, deer or bear meat, or wild turkey, for breakfast, dinner, and supper, if he could get it. His text was always ready, "Behold, the Lamb of God." This was old-fashioned Methodist preacher fare and fortune.[25]

This was borne out in the case of a British evangelist named George Cutting. One day while bicycling through an English village, Cutting felt impressed to shout out the words, "Behold! the Lamb of God who takes away the sin of the world!" Returning to the village six months later to evangelize door-to-door, he asked a particular woman if she was saved. "Oh yes!" she exclaimed. "Six months ago I was in great distress about the salvation of my soul. I pleaded for God's help. Then a voice cried, 'Behold! The Lamb of God who takes away the sin of the world!'"

∽

> *This Lamb is Christ, the soul's great Friend,*
> *The Lamb of God, our Savior;*
> *Him God the Father chose to send*
> *To gain for us His favor.*
>
> —PAUL GERHARDT, 1648

THE WORD

In the beginning was the Word, and the Word
was with God, and the Word was God.

—JOHN 1:1

IT TOOK THREE BIBLES TO BRING HIM TO CHRIST. DR. BORIS P. Dotsenko recalls growing up an atheist in the Soviet Union. One afternoon, recovering from a bout of pneumonia, he wandered into his grandfather's barn and discovered a Bible hidden behind the hay. This was a forbidden book, but Boris found himself reading it. He was struck by John 1:1: "In the beginning was the Word, and the Word was with God, and the Word was God."

"Here was a very clear statement of what was at the beginning, underneath everything," he said. "But it completely contradicted everything that I had been taught." The words from John 1 stayed with him as he studied at the University of Kiev. Later, working on his master's degree at the University of Leningrad, Boris found another Bible in an unlikely place: the study of the world-famous Soviet scientist, Dr. Jakov Frenkel. He was impressed that a great scientist read God's Word.

After earning his doctorate, Boris was assigned to the Academy of Sciences of the Soviet Union, where he worked on intercontinental and space rocket research. While attending a conference in Canada, he discovered his third Bible in his hotel room. It opened to John 1:1, and he instantly remembered the words that had impressed him twenty-two years earlier. As a result, he gave his life to Christ and eventually became a clear, compassionate witness for Christ to the scientific community.[26]

The verse that so moved Dr. Boris Dotsenko is a profound philosophical statement. "The Word" is the Greek term *Logos:* Communication. Self-expression. Saying. This special Word preexisted and was present at the beginning of the universe. He was *with* God and He *was* God. At the right moment, *Logos* "became flesh and dwelt among us, and we beheld His glory, the glory as of the only begotten of the Father" (John 1:14).

Jesus is God's ultimate communication to this earth. He is the revelation of all that God inherently is.

Come, Thou incarnate Word,
Gird on Thy mighty sword, our prayer attend!
Come, and Thy people bless, and give Thy Word success,
Spirit of holiness, on us descend!

— ANONYMOUS, 1757

THAT ETERNAL LIFE

That which was from the beginning, which we have heard,
which we have seen with our eyes, which we have looked upon,
and our hands have handled, concerning the Word of life—
that life was manifested, and we have seen,
and bear witness, and declare to you that eternal life.

—1 JOHN 1:1–2

THE APOSTLE JOHN MADE TWO ENORMOUS POINTS HERE:
First, Jesus is God Himself, the Word of Life—the Eternal Life that
was with the Father in the beginning. Second, Jesus is also human. "I
have touched Him," said John. "I have heard His voice with my ears,
felt His flesh with my hands, seen His body with my eyes."

To diminish any part of our theology of Jesus Christ is to bankrupt
our own souls.

It is the eternal nature of Christ that comforts us in the face of
death. Jesus said, "A little while longer and the world will see Me no
more, but you will see Me. Because I live, you will live also" (John
14:19). In other words: "Because I am rising from the dead to resume
eternity, I can bestow life after death. I can and will give you eternal
life."

Every other system of philosophy falters at this point. There is no
answer to death apart from the resurrection of Christ. The Swiss
philosopher and poet, Henri-Frederic Amiel, wrote: "Melancholy is
at the bottom of everything, just as at the end of all rivers is the sea.
Can it be otherwise in a world where nothing lasts, where all that we
have loved or shall love must die?"

As Francis Schaeffer said, "There is no other sufficient philosophical answer. . . . There is only one philosophy, one religion, that fills
this need in all the world's thought . . . and it is the Judaeo-Christian
God—not just an abstract concept, but rather that this God is really

there. He really exists. It is not that this is the best answer to existence; it is the only answer."[27]

In the preface of *Brave New World*, philosopher Aldous Huxley wrote that we should judge all things as if we saw them from our deathbeds. From their deathbeds, Christians see the Lord. We see everlasting life. We see the city whose builder and maker is God. We see the mountains of eternity. We see the face of Jesus. He is That Eternal Life.

Crown Him the Lord of life, who triumphed o'er the grave,
And rose victorious in the strife for those He came to save.
His glories now we sing, Who died, and rose on high,
Who died eternal life to bring, and lives that death may die.

—MATTHEW BRIDGES, 1852

THE TRUE BREAD FROM HEAVEN

"Our fathers ate the manna in the desert; as it is written, 'He gave them bread from heaven to eat.'" Then Jesus said to them, "Most assuredly, I say to you, Moses did not give you the bread from heaven, but My Father gives you the true bread from heaven." . . . Then they said to Him, "Lord, give us this bread always."

—JOHN 6:31–34

FOR FORTY YEARS, GOD FED THE ISRAELITES WITH EXOTIC bread known as *manna*—a Hebrew word meaning "What is it?" It was readily available, easy to prepare, pleasant to the taste; and it contained everything the human body needed: every vitamin, mineral, enzyme, and so on. It kept an entire nation alive for years in the midst of a blazing desert.

From Exodus 16 we learn that manna appeared on the ground with the dew, was flat and flaky, melted in the sun, was white in color, and was described as bread, though I believe this means it had the capacity to be *made into* bread. It could be prepared in a variety of ways—by baking or boiling, for example. It tasted like wafers made with honey.

The people gathered it, then ground it in a hand mill or crushed it in a mortar. They cooked it in a pot or made it into cakes. It tasted like something made with olive oil. Based on these descriptions, I believe manna was like a kind of grain, perhaps flat like oats and small like coriander. It was the world's most perfect food.

The enemies of Jesus had this in mind as they heard of Jesus' miracle of multiplying the loaves and fish in John 6. Jesus had taken a little boy's lunch and used it to feed five thousand. His critics said, in effect, "That's nothing! Moses fed us with manna from heaven."

Jesus replied, "My Father gives you the true bread from heaven. For the bread of God is He who comes down from heaven and gives life to the world. . . . I am the bread of life" (John 6:32–33, 35).

His Johannine Names

Jesus was comparing Himself to ancient manna in two ways: First, He came down from heaven. Second, His presence sustains our lives. He is a heaven-sent source of everything we need to remain inwardly and eternally healthy. His very body—broken for us like a loaf of unleavened bread—provides eternal salvation. He is the True Bread from Heaven sent down to us like manna from the heavenly Father.

"Lord, give us this bread always."

A precious food is this indeed—
It never fails us in our need—
A heavenly manna for our soul.
Until we safely reach our goal.

—HAQUIN SPEGEL, 1686

THE LIGHT OF THE WORLD

Then Jesus spoke to them again, saying, "I am the
light of the world. He who follows Me shall not walk
in darkness, but have the light of life."

—JOHN 8:12

IN THE VILLAGE OF HOLSBY BRUNN, SWEDEN, IS A ONE-
year Bible school, run by a group called the Torchbearers, that attracts
young people from across Europe and North America. Every year I
teach a course there, and every winter I'm enchanted by the tiny
lamps hanging in the windows of all the houses up and down the
roads. Every home is illumined by small lights suspended in the win-
dowsills. When I asked about it, I was told that it's a valiant attempt
to do the impossible—to replace the sun.

The long, dark winters depress the Scandinavians, and many of
them suffer from SAD—Seasonal Affective Disorder. In the middle
of winter, the sun barely comes up by late morning, and it retreats by
late afternoon. The little lights are like illumined sentries posted at
the windows of their homes to ward off the encroaching darkness
and to yield a cheerful glow to the inhabitants of the house.

Think of a world in which no sun is shining at all. It would be
frozen in a solid coat of eternal coldness, blackened in everlasting
darkness, and as lifeless as a spinning tomb.

Think of a soul in which the light of Jesus Christ is unwelcome.
That person may string up little artificial lights like a man hanging
holiday lights from the rafters, yet under the eaves, the heart is all cold
and dark and frozen.

Jesus said, "I have come as a light into the world, that whoever believes in Me should not abide in darkness" (John 12:44-46). He shines
from within, and every corner and crevice of our emotions and
thoughts are coated in the warmth and light of His indwelling presence. This is one of the greatest themes of the fourth Gospel.

—◌ *In Him was life, and the life was the light of men (1:4)*

—◌ *Light has come into the world (3:19)*

—◌ *I am the light of the world (8:12)*

—◌ *As long as I am in the world, I am the light of the world (9:5)*

—◌ *Believe in the light, that you may become sons of light (12:36)*

Missionary E. Stanley Jones once said, "When I met Christ, I felt that I had swallowed sunshine." Isn't that the way we should feel every day? He shines the light and warmth of Himself into the windows of our soul—emotionally, spiritually, mentally, and even physically. Even in the dead of winter.

> *Come to the light, 'tis shining for thee;*
> *Sweetly the light has dawned upon me.*
> *Once I was blind, but now I can see:*
> *The Light of the world is Jesus!*

—PHILIP BLISS, 1875

THE DOOR OF THE SHEEP

Then Jesus said to them again, "Most assuredly,
I say to you, I am the door of the sheep."

—JOHN 10:7

IN 1916, ANEES T. BAROODY, A LEBANESE SHEPHERD, PRI-
vately published a little volume entitled *The Syrian Shepherd: What an*
Oriental Thinks of the Shepherd-Life of the Bible. I don't recall how I
acquired a copy, but it has been an enormous help to me in understanding the nature of biblical shepherding. In describing the daily
routine of a shepherd on the heights of Lebanon, for example, Baroody said something that helps me envision Christ as the Door of the
Sheep:

> *Our shepherd . . . returns home with his flock in the evening. His lit-*
> *tle village, nestling most restfully on the shoulders of a Lebanon hill,*
> *in the midst of a fascinating circle of ancient pines and oaks, looks*
> *from the adjacent seacoast like a piece of new paradise. The sheep,*
> *being tired, are led straight to the fold, where they are counted and*
> *left to rest. Then the shepherd goes home, washes his face and feet, and*
> *takes supper. . . .*
>
> *Early in the evening our shepherd returns to his sheep, spreads his*
> *bed across the door of the fold, lays his heavy rod by his side, and sings*
> *himself quietly and happily to sleep.*
>
> *Does this not remind us of the meaning of Christ when He said, "I*
> *am the door"? During the long silence of the Lebanon night the*
> *wolves may prowl around the fold, the thieves may peep over the*
> *wall, but the mere presence of the shepherd at the door is sufficient to*
> *hold all the enemies of the sheep at bay. . . .*
>
> *As long as the Good Shepherd is at the door of [our] hearts, yea,*
> *rather in [our] hearts, [we] are safer than the stars in their courses and*
> *need not worry.*

Jesus said, "I am the door of the sheep. All who ever came before Me are thieves and robbers, but the sheep do not hear them. I am the door. If anyone enters by Me, he will be saved, and will go in and out and find pasture" (John 10:7–9).

As our Door, Jesus gives us access into all the blessings of God, and He provides security in the night watches of the soul.

O precious word that Jesus said! Behold, I am the Door;
And all who enter in by Me have life forevermore.
Have life forevermore, have life forevermore,
And all who enter in by Me have life forevermore.

—FANNY CROSBY, 1886

I AM

Jesus said to them, "Most assuredly, I say to you,
before Abraham was, I AM."
Then they took up stones to throw at Him;
but Jesus hid Himself and went out of the temple,
going through the midst of them, and so passed by.

—JOHN 8:58–59

THIS CHAPTER BEGINS AND ENDS WITH A NEAR-STONING. AT the beginning of John 8, the scribes and Pharisees brought to Jesus a woman charged with adultery. The Pharisees reminded Him that the law of Moses commanded that such offenders be stoned. Instead, Jesus forgave her, turning to those around Him and saying, "I am the light of the world" (v. 12).

The Pharisees were none too happy. There followed a tense exchange in which the name Abraham kept coming up. The Pharisees claimed they were children of Abraham, and they were stunned when Jesus uttered an even greater claim: "Your father Abraham rejoiced to see My day, and saw it and was glad" (v. 56)

The Jews asked scornfully, "You're not yet fifty years old, and have You seen Abraham?" (v. 57).

Jesus said to them, "Most assuredly, I say to you, before Abraham was, I AM" (v. 58). At that, the Pharisees forgot all about the woman, reaching for stones instead to throw at Jesus.

They understood Jesus was making three claims that seemed blasphemous to them. First, He was claiming to be God Himself, I AM being a famous Old Testament name for God. The Lord told Moses in Exodus 3:14: "I AM WHO I AM. . . . Thus you shall say to the children of Israel, 'I AM has sent me to you.'" This title implies God's eternal self-existence.

Second, Jesus was claiming preexistence. He had been alive before

His birth, even predating Abraham. As God, He had existed from eternity past.

Third, He was an even greater figure than their father Abraham—the national hero of the Jewish people.

We face the same choice as the Pharisees. We can either stone Him or enthrone Him. Either reject Him as a fraud, or we give Him the keys of the kingdom of our hearts. Which do you choose?

~⚬~

To God and to the Lamb, I will sing, I will sing;
To God and to the Lamb, I will sing.
To God and to the Lamb Who is the great "I Am";
While millions join the theme, I will sing, I will sing;
While millions join the theme, I will sing.

—ALEXANDER MEANS, U.D.

THE WAY

Jesus said to him, "I am the way, the truth, and the life.
No one comes to the Father except through Me."

—JOHN 14:6

JESUS WAS RESPONDING HERE TO THOMAS'S QUESTION: "Lord, we do not know where You are going, and how can we know the way?" (v. 5). In response, our Lord issued His strongest words about the exclusivity of the gospel: Jesus came to give the life, to speak the truth, and to provide the Way—the one and only Way—to heaven.

This isn't a popular message, and Christianity is under intense attack on this very issue in our pluralistic world. "You're close-minded and intolerant," our critics say. "Jesus works for you, but Buddha works just as well for someone else, and still others find their religion in Mohammad. All these roads lead eventually to the same destination."

It isn't possible to hold that philosophy while believing the Bible. The two are mutually excusive. Here's the Bible's perspective on this question:

⟡ *Nor is there salvation in any other, for there is no other name under heaven given among men by which we must be saved. (Acts 4:12)*

⟡ *No one comes to the Father except through Me. (John 14:6)*

⟡ *For there is one God and one Mediator between God and men, the Man Christ Jesus, who gave Himself a ransom for all. (1 Timothy 2:5–6)*

⟡ *For no other foundation can anyone lay than that which is laid, which is Jesus Christ. (1 Corinthians 3:11)*

⌐ How shall we escape if we neglect so great a salvation?
(Hebrews 2:3)

If God could have redeemed the human race without shedding the blood of His precious Son, He surely would have done so. If He could have sent a religious teacher to save the world by ethical teaching alone, He would have. But neither Buddha, Confucius, Zoroaster, Mohammed, nor any other founder of a religion ever claimed to pay the penalty for the sins of the world. They couldn't even pay for their own sins, and their tired corpses are smoldering in the grave to this day.

Only Christ died and rose again for the sins of the world. This narrow, exclusive, blood-bought message is designed to fit perfectly into that vacuum in the middle of our hearts.

Thou art the Way: to Thee alone
From sin and death we flee;
And he who would the Father seek
Must seek Him, Lord, by Thee.

—GEORGE W. DOANE, 1824

THE TRUTH

I am the way, the truth, and the life.

—JOHN 14:6

"MEN OCCASIONALLY STUMBLE OVER THE TRUTH," SAID WINston Churchill, "but most of them pick themselves up and hurry off as if nothing had happened."

Truth is that which perfectly corresponds to reality. Truth does exist, and it is absolute. It is grounded in facts that never change, and it provides consistent intellectual and moral scaffolding for the universe in general and for our own lives in particular. It is codified in the Scripture and perfectly represented in the person of Jesus Christ.

Many people, of course, try to deny all this. In an age of relative values, most pundits are either quoting Pontius Pilate, who scornfully asked, "What is truth?" (John 18:38) or echoing Adolf Hitler, who claimed, "There is no such thing as truth."

I'd advise all such doubters to read the Gospel of John, for truth was one of his best words and highest concepts. "The Word became flesh," says John, "and dwelt among us, and we beheld His glory, the glory as of the only begotten of the Father, full of grace and truth. . . . The law was given through Moses, but grace and truth came through Jesus Christ." Jesus Himself said, "If you abide in My Word, you are My disciples indeed. And you shall know the truth, and the truth shall make you free" (1:14, 17, 8:31–32).

Spiritual realities are just as sure and certain as physical laws and scientific fact. Moral truth is just as solid and inflexible as the dimensions of time and space. We ignore any zone of truth at our own peril. Jesus went on to say, "[I am] a Man who has told you the truth . . . [The devil] does not stand in the truth, because there is no truth in him. . . . But because I tell you the truth, you do not believe Me" (John 8:40, 44-45).

By letting the Truth Himself and His trustworthy Word dwell

richly within us, we are sanctified, cleansed, set apart, equipped, strengthened, enlightened, guided, nourished, and set on a course leading to everlasting life.

⚜

Jesus, my Way, my Truth, my Life,
My God, my All in all;
At Thy blest feet, in humble love,
And lowly fear, I fall.

—WILLIAM MASON, EIGHTEENTH CENTURY

THE LIFE

I am the way, the truth, and the life.

—John 14:6

In calling Himself "The Life," Jesus meant, among other things, that He Himself was the source, center, and secret of every happy life that ever lived. He alone gives us life both abundant and eternal.

Take, for instance, James Wilson. It's a shame Hollywood has never discovered James. His story would make an epic movie. Born in the mid-1700s, he was one of nineteen children. His father, a ship captain, took him as a boy to sea, and James grew up amid vulgar scoundrels. He served in the British Navy, then became a trader on the high seas. When he was captured by a brutal North African pirate named Hyder Ali, he knew he was facing a fate worse than death, especially when he ended up in a brutal French prison in Cuddalore.

In a desperate leap for freedom, he jumped from the ramparts of the prison into a river teeming with alligators. He was captured by Hyder Ali's horsemen, stripped, bound, and marched thirty-five miles under the blazing sun. Blistered and bleeding, he staggered into the prison and was offered a pardon if he would convert to Islam. Wilson, who was an irreligious Deist, refused to do so.

For two years, Wilson was fastened to another man and bound with irons weighing thirty-two pounds. The two prisoners were left exposed, and the nights became so cold they dug a hole in the ground and tried to cover themselves with dirt. To stave off starvation, Wilson ate the white ants that scurried on the ground.

Finally liberated by the British, Wilson returned to his trading ventures and gained a fortune that allowed him to retire at age thirty-four on a beautiful estate in England. One night, an old seafaring buddy came to see him, bringing along a preacher—Reverend John Griffin. "In three hours' conversation," Wilson later wrote, "John

Griffin convinced me of the weakness of my belief in deism and planted in my mind certain truths which led to my conversion. The text which he used with convincing effect was John 14:6."

James Wilson went on to become a powerful force in gospel expansion, purchasing a ship for transporting missionaries to the South Pacific and laboring there so effectively that his later adventures as a missionary eclipsed his earlier ones as a pagan.

His great secret? "Dwell much in John 14:6," he once said. "Jesus is the only source of life abundant for discouraged Christians and the only source of eternal life and hope for a degraded race."[28]

❧

O Christ, the Way, the Truth, the Life,
Show me the living way,
That in the tumult and the strife,
I may not go astray.

—GEORGE L. SQUIER, 1907

THE MAN

Then Jesus came out, wearing the crown of thorns
and the purple robe. And Pilate said to them, "Behold the Man!"

—JOHN 19:5

"BEHOLD THE MAN!" THE LATIN VERSION OF PILATE'S FA-
mous words is *Ecce Homo,* words that have become engraved on
Christian history and in Western art, signifying a type of devotional
image that depicts Jesus after His scourging. The Savior's face is often
battered and bloody, and his brow is crowned with thorns. If one
travels across Europe visiting art museums, the title *Ecce Homo* appears beneath many paintings of this scene. It was a prominent subject for artists, especially in the fifteenth through the seventeenth
centuries.[29]

Years ago, a teenage hymnist was moved by Domenico Feti's painting *Ecce Homo* in the art museum in Düsseldorf, Germany. The
work inspired Francis Ridley Havergal to write a hymn based on the
painting's caption: "I have done this for you; what have you done for
Me?"

Havergal wrote: "I gave my life for thee, My precious blood I shed,
/ That thou might'st ransomed be, and quickened from the dead; / I
gave, I gave my life for thee, what hast thou given for me?"

Interestingly, over a hundred years before, another young person
had been deeply stirred while studying the same painting. In the early
1700s a young German nobleman named Nikolaus Ludwig von
Zinzendorf visited the art museum in Düsseldorf and was transfixed
by Feti's *Ecce Homo* and its convicting caption. The young count was
moved to make a full surrender of his life to Christ, and he went on to
become one of the most powerful Christian leaders of the eighteenth
century, establishing a Moravian community at Herrnhut and
launching a new era of Protestant missions that changed the shape of
Christian history.

Would your life be changed if you came face to face with the probing eyes of Jesus Christ? All this He did for you. What have you done for Him? Behold the Man.

"Behold," they say, "Behold the man
Whom providence relieved;
The man so dangerously beset,
So wondrously retrieved!"

—NAHUM TATE AND NICHOLAS BRANDY, 1698

THE ADVOCATE

My little children, these things I write to you, so that you may not sin.
And if anyone sins, we have an Advocate with the Father,
Jesus Christ the righteous.

— 1 JOHN 2:1

THIS VERSE GIVES US FOUR WONDERFUL ASPECTS OF CHRIS-
tian living—we have a great adversary, a great adventure, a great advantage, and a great Advocate.

Our great adversary is sin, a word that occurs twice in this verse.
The Greek term John used was *hamartan,* which means "to miss, not
to hit, to fall short, to do wrong." The tendency to sin is so interwoven
into our human nature that we sin continually in ways known and
unknown.

Yet there's also a great adventure. It *is* possible to live in consistent
victory over known sin. In this verse, John desired that we not sin. We
don't have to keep falling into Satan's traps, and it isn't necessary to
yield continually to temptation. Though we'll never be perfect in this
life, sin should not have dominion over us. There is a higher, deeper
Christian life that increasingly experiences victory over daily sin.

Third, we have a great advantage—God's Word. "These things I
write to you," said John, "so that you may not sin." As we identify our
particular weaknesses and temptations, it's possible to find verses in
the Bible that attack those specific issues with bare knuckles. By
memorizing and utilizing those verses, we have a two-edged sword
in our fight. God's Word hidden in our hearts is our best ammunition
against Satan.

Finally, we have a great Advocate. On those occasions when we do
fail and fall, Jesus Christ represents us before the throne of holiness,
pleading His own blood on our behalf. The reason we can forgive
ourselves of past mistakes and regrets is simply this: His forgiveness is
all-encompassing, total, eternal, finished, and final. The blood of

Christ so thoroughly expunges our sins that it is itself a sin to keep bringing them up. They're gone. As Eliza Hewitt put it, "I need no other argument, I need no other plea; / It is enough that Jesus died, and that He died for me."

My Advocate appears
For my defense on high;
The Father bows His ears,
And lays His thunder by:
Not all that hell or sin can say
Shall turn His heart, His love away.

—Isaac Watts, 1709

THE PROPITIATION FOR OUR SINS

And He Himself is the propitiation for our sins,
and not for ours only but also for the whole world.

— 1 John 2:2

A PRECOCIOUS LITTLE GIRL, ABOUT TEN, BOUNDED UP TO ME on Sunday night posing a question that caught me short: "Pastor Rob, what does *propitiation* mean?"

"Well," I said, "let me see. . . ." I stalled a moment, then stammered out a reasonable answer for a ten-year old; but I left the church that night asking myself, *What* does *that word mean?*

The newer translations don't even bother to use it, assuming, I suppose, modern audiences aren't interested in such theological jargon. They render the verse "atoning sacrifice." The actual term, however, has a profound meaning: a sacrifice designed to avert wrath.

This assumes God is wrathful—and that's an assumption in which we should rejoice. I'm glad our Lord is a God of wrath, for there'd be something wrong if He could look dispassionately at evil. In reading the accounts of survivors of death camps or the victims of torture in totalitarian lands, I feel a stab of pain twist in my stomach. If God could observe those same atrocities without indignation, He'd be imperfect.

The problem is that some of the same evil that motivates the tyrants is inside of you and me. Our bloodstreams are all infected with sin. "There is none righteous, no not one; / There is none who understands; / There is none who seeks after God" (Rom. 3:10–11). The pure and just wrath of God targets us all, "for our God is a consuming fire" (Heb. 12:29).

Only one substance in heaven and earth averts the wrath of God: the crimson blood of our Lord Jesus, "whom God set forth as a propitiation by His blood, through faith" (Rom. 3:25). "Therefore, in all things He had to be made like His brethren, that He might be a merciful and faithful High Priest in things pertaining to God, to make propitiation for the sins of the people" (Heb. 2:17). "In this is love, not that we loved God, but that He loved us and sent His Son to be the propitiation for our sins" (1 John 4:10).

Today, try something new. Bow your head and use that long, cumbersome, theological word in prayer: "Thank You, Jesus, for being the propitiation for my sins! Thank You for mercy!"

Depth of mercy! Can there be
Mercy still reserved for me?
Can my God His wrath forbear,
Me, the chief of sinners, spare?

Jesus speaks, and pleads His blood!
He disarms the wrath of God;
Now my Father's mercies move,
Justice lingers into love.

—CHARLES WESLEY, 1740

THE RESURRECTION AND THE LIFE

I am the resurrection and the life. He who believes in Me, though he
may die, he shall live. And whoever lives and believes in
Me shall never die.

—JOHN 11:25–26

WHEN THE GREAT BRITISH PREACHER MARTYN LLOYD-JONES
was dying of cancer, a physician friend tried to prescribe a sedative to
make him more comfortable. Lloyd-Jones, too weak to speak, vigor-
ously shook his head. He wanted nothing to dull his mind. His friend,
quoting an old hymn, said it grieved him to see his patient "weary,
worn, and sad." That was too much for Lloyd-Jones, who mustered
all his strength to whisper an adamant protest: "Not sad! Not sad!"

Just before his death, he managed to scribble a note to his beloved
wife and family: "Do not pray for healing. Do not hold me back from
glory."[30]

Lloyd-Jones understood this marvelous title for Christ: the Resurrection and the Life. Jesus spoke it in the village of Bethany, about
two miles from Jerusalem on the southeastern slopes of the Mount of
Olives. Today Bethany has been swallowed up within the city limits
of greater Jerusalem, but you can still see the alleged tomb of Lazarus.

There's a good chance it really is his tomb, for the traditions surrounding it are very old. Eusebius, writing in the fourth century, said
that the tomb of Lazarus was being shown to pilgrims in his day; and
in the late fourth century Saint Jerome made mention of a church
built nearby. The ruins of that church have been found near this ancient tomb. I myself have visited there on two occasions.

Jesus wasn't in Bethany when Lazarus fell ill, but, hearing the
news, He uttered a cryptic word: "This sickness is not unto death, but
for the glory of God" (John 11:4). The New International Version
says, "This sickness will not end in death" (NIV).

"Will not *end* in death": That's one of the greatest verses in the Bible for Christians facing bleak prospects with their health. Lazarus *did* die, but Jesus arrived bearing three simple words: "Lazarus, come forth!" The illness *included* death, but it did not *end* there.

Jesus of Nazareth is the Resurrection and the Life. Those who believe in Him, though they die, yet shall they live. "And whoever lives and believes in [Him] shall never die."

This will not end the way you fear,
Though shadows linger near,
I am the Resurrection Life,
My voice is heard above the strife:
Come forth! Lift up your hearts! Be glad!
Not sad! Not sad!

THE VINE

*I am the vine, you are the branches. He who abides in Me,
and I in him, bears much fruit; for without Me you can do nothing.*

—JOHN 15:5

THIS IS THE LAST OF OUR LORD'S GREAT I AM STATEMENTS
as recorded in John's Gospel. Jesus used the analogy of a grapevine to
teach us vital secrets of the Christian life.

The essential lesson is we're to bear fruit, more fruit, and much
fruit (vv. 2, 5). The "fruit" to which He refers is the character and
qualities of the Lord Jesus. A remarkable list of nine elements in the
Bible provides a pen-portrait of Jesus' character and personality. It's
found in Galatians 5:22, and the nine elements are called "the fruit of
the Spirit."

Not "*fruits* of the Spirit." The picture isn't an assortment of apples
on a tree, but a cluster of grapes on a vine. They grow proportionally
to one another. It's a total personality package: love, joy, peace, patience, kindness, goodness, gentleness, faithfulness, and self-control.

Jesus possessed infinite amounts of love, for example—He cared
deeply for others and incessantly sought to meet their needs. He dis-
played unshakable peace. He was patient, even when His disciples
grated on His nerves. He was a masterpiece of self-control.

Those nine qualities should be developing in our lives all the time,
like grapes maturing on a healthy vine. We should be growing in
Christlikeness.

How does that happen? Not so much by our own efforts. The secret is abiding in the Vine—maintaining a close daily relationship
with Him. Staying in His Word. Praying. Drawing near to Him.
Practicing His presence. Trusting Him with the frustrations of life.

As we do those things, the invisible "sap" of the Holy Spirit flows
through Christ—the Vine—into us, the branches, and gradually
produces the fruit. We may not notice it, but those around us will.

Day by day, year after year, we'll be growing more loving, more joyful, more peaceful, more patient, more like Him.

Are you abiding in Christ today?

Chief of sinners though I be,
Jesus shed His blood for me;
Died that I might live on high,
Died that I might never die;
As the branch is to the vine,
I am His, and He is mine.

—WILLIAM McCOMB, 1864

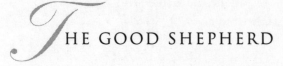

THE GOOD SHEPHERD

I have come that they may have life, and that they may have it more abundantly. I am the good shepherd. The good shepherd gives His life for the sheep.

—John 10:10–11

ABUNDANT IS ONE OF THE SHEPHERD'S FAVORITE WORDS. IT means "more than enough, overflow, vast amounts, excessive supplies." Picture endless acres of green pastures, plenteous ponds of still waters, unlimited supplies of grain, oil, and blue skies with no boundaries. Our Good Shepherd is an abundant provider.

- He gives abundant pardon:

  The LORD is longsuffering and abundant in mercy, forgiving iniquity and transgression. (Numbers 14:18)
  He will abundantly pardon. (Isaiah 55:7)

- He gives abundant blessings as we give Him our tithes and offerings:

  Since the people began to bring the offerings into the house of the LORD, we have had enough to eat and have plenty left, for the LORD has blessed His people; and what is left is this great abundance. (2 Chronicles 31:10)

- His kindness is abundant:

  You are God,
  Ready to pardon,
  Gracious and merciful,
  Slow to anger,
  Abundant in kindness. (Nehemiah 9:17)

- His blessings are abundant:

  How precious is your lovingkindess, O God!

*Therefore the children of men put their trust under the shadow of
Your wings.
They are abundantly satisfied. (Psalm 37:7–8)
You crown the year with your goodness,
And Your paths drip with abundance. (Psalm 65:11)*

—↻ His peace is abundant:

*The meek shall inherit the earth,
And shall delight themselves in the abundance of peace.
(Psalm 37:11)
I will heal them and reveal to them the abundance of peace and
truth. (Jeremiah 33:6)*

—↻ His answers to prayer are abundant:

*Now to Him who is able to do exceedingly abundantly above all
that we ask or think. . . . (Ephesians 3:20)*

—↻ His Spirit is abundant:

*The Holy Spirit, whom He poured out on us abundantly through
Jesus Christ our Savior. . . . (Titus 3:5–6)*

—↻ His hope is abundant:

*Blessed be the God and Father of our Lord Jesus Christ, who
according to His abundant mercy has begotten us again to a living
hope through the resurrection of Jesus Christ from the dead, to an
inheritance incorruptible and undefiled and that does not fade away,
reserved in heaven for you. (1 Peter 1:3–4)*

"I will abundantly bless," says the Good Shepherd. "Let your soul
delight itself in abundance. . . . I have come that [you might] have
life . . . more abundantly" (Ps. 132:15; Isa. 55:2; John 10:10).

*I praise and thank Thee, Lord, my God,
For Thine abundant blessing
Which heretofore Thou hast bestowed
And I am still possessing.*

—ÄMILIE JULIANE, 1699

THE SERPENT IN THE WILDERNESS

And as Moses lifted up the serpent in the wilderness, even so
must the Son of Man be lifted up, that whoever believes in
Him should not perish but have eternal life.

—JOHN 3:14–15

THIS IS THE PREAMBLE TO THE MOST FAMOUS AND BELOVED
verse in the Bible—John 3:16. It harkens back to a strange story
found in Numbers 21. The Israelites, traveling through the desert,
had grown impatient and ill-mannered, railing against Moses and
complaining against the Lord. "There is no bread!" they carped.
"There is no water! And we detest this miserable food!" (v. 5 NIV).

As judgment, "the LORD sent venomous snakes among them; they
bit the people, and many Israelites died." So great was the panic that
Moses confronted God about it in prayer. The Lord told him to make
a bronze snake and to lift it high upon a pole: "Anyone who is bitten
can look at it and live" (vv. 6, 8 NIV).

In speaking to Nicodemus in John 3, Jesus claimed to be the fulfillment of that type. The venomous serpent called *sin* has bitten all humanity. All are dying. But Jesus Christ, becoming sin for us, was
lifted up on the cross, and by looking on Him in faith, we are healed.
"As Moses lifted up the serpent in the wilderness, even so must the
Son of Man be lifted up, that whoever believes in Him should not perish but have eternal life. For God so loved the world that He gave His
only begotten Son, that whosoever believes in Him should not perish
but have everlasting life" (vv. 14–16).

"Oh that precious word, 'whosoever,'" cried Charles Spurgeon one
Sunday. "Remember there is the same Christ for big sinners as for lit-
tle sinners; the same Christ for grey heads as for babes; the same
Christ for poor as for rich; the same Christ for chimney sweeps as for

monarchs; the same Christ for prostitutes as for saints: Whosoever . . .
whosoever looks to Christ shall live."[31]

As when the Hebrew prophet raised
The brazen serpent high,
The wounded looked and straight were cured,
The people ceased to die.

So from the Savior on the cross
A healing virtue flows;
Who looks to Him with lively faith
Is saved from endless woes.

—ISAAC WATTS, 1709

$\mathcal{T}$EACHER

You call me Teacher . . . for so I am.

—JOHN 13:13

THE MASTER TEACHER ONCE TAUGHT A LESSON TWENTY-four feet long.

His disciples had been jockeying for position and nursing their egos, and Jesus had devoted teaching time to this issue. But even in the Upper Room on the eve of the cross, the little band was out of sorts. Quietly rising from the table, Jesus brought the murmurings to a halt by removing His outer garments—some commentators say He stripped to the loincloth of a slave—and began washing their feet. This was a customary act of hospitality in biblical times when transportation was by foot in sandals along dusty roadways. Servants usually performed this act, but to the embarrassment of the Twelve, Jesus took that role upon Himself.

When He came to Peter, He met resistance, but Jesus responded firmly: "If I do not wash you, you have no part with Me." With typical rashness, Peter said, "Lord, not my feet only, but also my hands and head!" Jesus replied, "He who is bathed needs only to wash his feet, but is completely clean" (John 13:8–10).

Having finished the twenty-four feet, Jesus rose, replaced His robe, and resumed His seat at the head of the table.

His words to Peter indicate there was more to His actions than met the foot. In one twenty-minute lesson, Jesus encapsulated His entire mission. This foot-washing was a miniaturized version of His Passion. Just as a drop of water contains all the life of a pond, this one act of our Lord was a microcosm of His whole ministry.

Think of it: the Almighty Son, arrayed in splendor, rose from His heavenly place, laid aside His garments of glory, took the form of a servant, descended to ground zero, and humbly cleansed His squabbling, sinful children. He washes us from soul-destroying sin (head and hands and heart) as well as from the daily "dust on our feet" that can strain our fellowship with God. Then He arose, replaced His regalia, and resumed His place of honor at heaven's throne.

The Teacher's lesson: our daily acts of humility—washing one another's feet—not only reflect His loving heart; they emulate His redemptive mission. "I have given you an example," He said, "that you should do as I have done to you" (John 8:15).

Have you been jealous of another? What can you humbly do for that one today?

Our great example Thou shalt be,
In washing Thy disciples' feet;
And as we follow Thy command,
Make Thou our fellowship complete.

—William Brickey, c. 1886

ABBI

Rabbi, we know that You are a teacher come from God.

—JOHN 3:2

I CAN USUALLY SPOT IMMATURITY IN SOMEONE ELSE, BUT seeing it in myself is another story. Immaturity is akin to stupidity, a condition that is obvious to everyone except the person exhibiting it. Whether it's a child having a tantrum, a student hitting the party circuit, a neighbor talking too much, or an executive in midlife crisis, immaturity blinds its victim to its own presence.

Most of our family problems stem from immaturity in all its manifested forms: overreacting, selfishness, pouting, pettiness, short tempers, and shortsightedness. Many church splits occur because of immaturity. Wars have raged due to immaturity on one or both sides.

Several times in the Gospels, Jesus is called *Rabbi,* a term of respect the Hebrews developed for their teachers. The word comes from the Hebrew term for "great," and it developed into a designation meaning "Great Teacher" or "My Master and Teacher." It was used by those who put themselves under the tutelage of another in order to learn, to grow, and to mature.

Ephesians 4:13 summarizes the Lord's desire for us. He wants "all of us to come to the unity of the faith and of the knowledge of the Son of God, to maturity, to the measure of the full stature of Christ" (NRSV).

How does Rabbi Jesus bring immature people to maturity? His *textbook* is the Scripture. As we study His Word each day, memorizing and meditating on its chapters and verses, He shows us where and how we need to mature.

His *classroom* is trouble. We do our best maturing when we're confronting the trials and tribulations of life.

His *tool* is time. The process of physical maturation doesn't occur overnight. A child grows so slowly that daily growth is virtually unobservable. But over the years, growth—or the lack of it—is obvious. Spiritual and emotional maturing is the same.

Let Rabbi Jesus be your Master Teacher, and don't despair. He knows how to bring us to the full measure of the stature of Christ.

⁓

More about Jesus let me learn,
More of His holy will discern;
Spirit of God, my teacher be,
Showing the things of Christ to me.

—ELIZA HEWITT, 1887

HE WHO COMES FROM HEAVEN

He who comes from heaven is above all.

—JOHN 3:31

THE THIRD CHAPTER OF THE GOSPEL OF JOHN contains several similar phrases for our Lord, all describing His precipitous descent from the realms of glory to the sphere of sin and suffering: "He who came down from heaven, that is, the Son of Man" (v. 13); "He who comes from above is above all" (v. 31); "He who comes from heaven is above all" (v. 31).

In a recent newsletter, missionary and college president George Murray wrote of the many holiday seasons he had spent overseas. He and his wife were missionaries in southern Europe for thirteen years. Not long after their arrival in Italy as rookie missionaries, the holidays approached and they faced their first Christmas away from home and family. They experienced genuine homesickness. They longed for familiar sights and sounds and smells—such as pumpkin pie and cranberries, which were unknown commodities in the Mediterranean basin where they lived. They missed their family gatherings. They missed their childhood traditions. They badly wanted to go home for Christmas.

Then one day as George was meditating on the meaning of Christmas, it hit him: Christmas isn't about *going* home. It's all about *leaving* home. That's what Jesus did. He deliberately left the comfort and security of His heavenly home to come to this sin-filled world. He was obeying His heavenly Father. He was representing God to this world. He said, "I have come down from heaven, not to do my will, but the will of Him who sent me. Behold, Here I am. I have come to do your will, O God" (see John 6:38).

With that realization renewed peace came to the Murray home, and a new appreciation for Christmas.

From heaven above to earth I come,
To bear good news to every home;
Glad tidings of great joy I bring,
Whereof I now will say and sing.

Welcome to earth, Thou noble Guest,
Through Whom e'en wicked men are blest!
Thou com'st to share our misery,
What can we render, Lord, to Thee!

Ah, dearest Jesus, holy Child,
Make Thee a bed, soft, undefiled,
Here in my poor heart's inmost shrine,
That I may evermore be Thine.

—MARTIN LUTHER, 1531

OUR PEACE

For He Himself is our peace.

—Ephesians 2:14

IN ITS CONTEXT, THIS VERSE IS REFERRING TO PEACE BE-
tween Jews and Gentiles who jointly made up the church in Ephesus.
Paul was emphasizing the universal availability of the gospel.
Though Jesus came as Jewish Messiah in fulfillment of Jewish
prophecies, He also died for the non-Jewish population of earth.
When Jews and Gentiles receive Christ as Savior, the wall between
them is broken down and they become part of one body. He Himself
is our peace—the cement that binds us together.

Adam and Eve's sin in the garden produced two tragic consequences: a separation occurred between them and a holy God, and
another barrier arose between Adam and Eve themselves. Suddenly
they became selfish, sinful, ego-centered, self-conscious, blaming one
another, capable of resentment, hatred, racism, and division.

The sad results of this were apparent in the next generation when
Cain killed his brother Abel. The basic problem wasn't between Cain
and Abel; it was between Cain and God. If Cain had gotten his heart
right with the Lord, things would have been different with his
brother.

Ephesians 2 teaches that the same Cross that reconciles us to God
also provides reconciliation with others, and the same Jesus who gives
us peace with God is also the basis of our harmony with one another.

What does that mean in practice? Whenever my wife and I get in a
fight, the real trouble is apt to be in me—my own heart out of tune
with the Lord. When I correct that, my difficulty with Katrina usually clears up by itself. The blockage in our marriage often resides in
my attitude, and it dissolves when I learn to abide in Christ.

Put another way, when my wife and I are both walking closely
with the Lord—having our quiet times, praying as we should, mem-

orizing and meditating on Scripture—we seldom have serious misunderstandings with each other.

I tell young couples before officiating their weddings that there are two rules for a good marriage and a happy home: we must (1) walk with the Master and (2) work on the marriage. As John put it, "If we walk in the light as He is in the light, we have fellowship with one another, and the blood of Jesus Christ His Son cleanses us from all sin" (1 John 1:7). He Himself is our peace—the tie that binds our hearts in Christian love.

Happy the home where Jesus' Name
Is sweet to every ear;
Where children early speak His fame,
And parents hold Him dear.

—HENRY WARE JR., N.D.

THE SAVIOR

For our citizenship is in heaven, from which we also eagerly wait for the Savior, the Lord Jesus Christ, who will transform our lowly body that it may be conformed to His glorious body, according to the working by which He is able even to subdue all things to Himself.

—Philippians 3:20–21

At 3:30 this morning my phone rang. A young man was sobbing on the other end. His dad had just died. Would I come? Arriving at the hospital, I found a grieving family, too numb to think, gathered around a lifeless body lying silently on the bed. The man, a wonderful Christian, had suffered for years with multiple diseases, and now his soul had slipped from its dilapidated dwelling and, under angelic escort, flown to be with Jesus.

I spoke to them of the future hope Christ gives us. That broken-down body had not taken its final breath. Philippians 3:20-21 tells us that Jesus is the Savior, not only of our souls, but of our physical bodies, too. The Greek term *sōtēr* means "one who rescues and delivers." At the coming resurrection the Savior will rescue and deliver our bodies from the ironclad grip of the grave, and they will be reconstituted and glorified according to the pattern of His resurrection body.

When Jesus rose from the dead, it was physically, literally, and bodily. "Behold My hands and My feet, that it is I Myself," He said. "Handle Me and see, for a spirit does not have flesh and bones as you see I have" (Luke 24:39).

He was solid, visible, touchable, three-dimensional. Yet His body was different. Ageless. Perfect. Healed. Incapable of pain or plague. Able to travel by some form of instant telekinesis. Appearing and disappearing at will. It was a perfect physical specimen of a mature, thirty-something man.

Philippians 3:20–21 promises that when He comes again, He will raise His children from the dead and transform their lowly bodies to conform to His glorious body. So if we want to know about our resurrection bodies, we just need to study the postresurrection accounts of Jesus.

Like His, our bodies will be ageless. Perfect. Healed. Incapable of pain or plague. I also think we'll all appear thirty-something—at the prime of life, like Adam and Eve at the creation or like Jesus at His resurrection—but that's just my own opinion.

At any rate, if we're raised physically from the grave with new and improved bodies, it only stands to reason that we'll have a physical and literal place to live. And we'll live forever with our eternal Savior—who not only saves our souls but our bodies as well.

Conformed to His own likeness,
May we so live and die,
That in the grave our bodies
In holy peace may lie;
And at the Resurrection
Forth from those graves may spring
Like to the glorious body
Of Christ, our Lord and King.

—CHRISTOPHER WORDSWORTH

THE SECOND MAN

The first man was of the earth, made of dust;
the second Man is the Lord from heaven.

— 1 Corinthians 15:47

According to Romans 5:14, Adam was a "type" of Christ—that is, he was one of those wonderful Old Testament foreshadows of Christ. There are remarkable similarities between the first man, Adam, and the Second Man, Christ, as the apostle Paul pointed out in two different chapters, Romans 5 and 1 Corinthians 15.

Consider these four parallels between these two epic figures.

One: both men entered the world differently from other mortals. The Almighty personally designed and created Adam; "He formed man from the dust of the ground, and breathed into his nostrils the breath of life" (Gen. 1:7). He entered the world as a fully grown, personally made, perfectly engineered human being. And Jesus Christ, too, entered the world in a way different from all other mortals. He was the perfect man, born of a virgin. "A body hast thou prepared me," He said in Hebrews 10:5 (KJV).

Two: both men were sinless. Have you ever gone for a walk on a winter's day when the whole landscape was covered with a fresh blanket of blinding white snow? The sun, bouncing against the sheer whiteness with powerful force, can almost put your eyes out. That's why we wear sunglasses when skiing. Jesus and Adam were both utterly, blindingly pure. No blemish, no shadow, no guilt of any kind.

Three: both men were tempted by the devil. Satan came to Adam and Eve, tempting them to disobey the one command God had given them. And in the Gospels, Satan came to Jesus Christ, the sinless Son of God, testing Him on the Mount of Temptation.

Four: both men became the head of a race. Adam became the head of the human race, and Jesus Christ became the head of the race of the redeemed, His children, His church. Through Adam came death, and through Christ came life.

There are also enormous contrasts, of course, as we'll see in the next devotion; but just consider how brilliantly the Lord unfolded His divine book. Thousands of years before Christ was born, God created a man as a prototype to the living Lord. As soon as we begin reading Genesis, we find at the dawning of human history a model for the Man of the ages.

⁂

Adam's likeness, Lord, efface;
Stamp Thy image in its place.
Second Adam from above,
Reinstate us in thy love.

—CHARLES WESLEY, 1739

CHRIST OUR PASSOVER

Therefore purge out the old leaven, that you may be a new lump, since you truly are unleavened. For indeed Christ, our Passover, was sacrificed for us.

— 1 CORINTHIANS 5:7

THIS TITLE FOR CHRIST IS ROOTED IN THE OLD TESTAMENT account of Passover. In the book of Exodus, Moses unleashed a series of destructive miracles against the Egyptian pharaoh who was holding the nation of Israel like a chained lion. The final weapon in Moses' arsenal was the killing of all the firstborn in Egypt. Silently the death angel penetrated every home, from clay huts to royal palaces, and the firstborn of every home died. It was symbolic of the death that is constantly enveloping the earth.

But there was a preventative — the blood of the lamb. In Exodus 12, Moses solemnly instructed the Israelites: "Every man shall take for himself a lamb. . . . Your lamb shall be without blemish. . . . Kill it. . . . And they shall take some of the blood and put it on the two doorposts and on the lintel of the houses when they eat it. . . . And when I see the blood, I will pass over you" (vv. 3, 5–7, 13).

To commemorate this never-to-be-forgotten night, the Israelites ate their Passover meal behind blood-stained doors. On the table with the lamb was unleavened bread. It was made without yeast for two reasons: (1) That very night the Israelites would flee captivity, and they didn't have time for the bread to rise. (2) Yeast in the Bible is symbolic of sin, because a little of it has the power to influence the whole lump of dough.

In 1 Corinthians 5:7, Paul considered the Passover a divine foreshadowing of Christ. He is the Lamb of God who shed His blood for us, and when we receive Him as our Lord and Savior, that blood is applied to our lives. When the wrath and judgment of God fall on earth, He will see the blood, and we're safe in His love.

As a result, we're to be diligent to keep our lives and churches free from the leaven of sin. For Christ is our Lamb, our Passover. When the Judge sees His blood on the doorposts of our lives, He will pass over us.

Now Christ our Passover is slain,
The Lamb of God without a stain;
His flesh, the true unleavened Bread,
Is freely offered in our stead.

— ANCIENT LATIN HYMN

OUR GREAT GOD AND SAVIOR

Looking for that blessed hope and glorious appearing of our great God and Savior Jesus Christ.

—TITUS 2:13

JESUS IS OUR GREAT GOD. HE'S OUR SAVIOR. HE HAD TO BE God in order to save us, and He saves us because of His godly impulses. When He returns in the clouds of splendor, we'll acknowledge Him in all His roles and titles, but we'll especially be thankful for Him as our great God and Savior, as our blessed hope for whom we're eagerly looking.

The other day in New Jersey I came across a story in an old book in a friend's library. It told of a fishing village in Scotland where the folks gathered to welcome home a boat that had been at sea. As the vessel neared shore, the men aboard gazed eagerly toward the dock where scattered groups of loved ones were waiting. The skipper, looking through his telescope, identified some of the women standing on the shore, saying, "I see Bill's wife. I see Tom's wife. There's David's wife."

One man was anxious because his wife wasn't there. No one met him. Leaving the dock with a heavy heart, he trudged home. There was a light in the window, and as he opened the door, his wife met him, saying, "Oh, John, I've been waiting for you."

"Yes," he said sadly, "but the other men's wives were *watching* for them."

This morning in my quiet time I was impressed with ten words I'd never seen before: "Eagerly wait for our Lord Jesus Christ to be revealed" (1 Cor. 1:7 NIV).

We're to *eagerly* wait. We should cast an impatient eye skyward, watching for the first glimpse of the sails of the Second Coming, looking for "that blessed hope and glorious appearing of our great God and Savior Jesus Christ."

Not many are doing that. Few did it when He came the first time. Aged Simeon was the exception, waiting for the Consolation of Israel (Luke 2:25). And elderly Anna spoke of His coming "to all who looked for redemption" (v. 38).

In the course of a typical day, how many people take even a moment to scan the clouds, wondering if it could be the day He returns? Paul spoke of the crown of righteousness to be given to all who love His appearing (2 Tim. 4:8). Hebrews 9:28 says, "To those who eagerly wait for Him He will appear a second time." Peter told us we should be "looking for and hastening the coming of the day of God . . . looking forward to these things" (2 Pet. 3:12, 14).

Let's learn the holy habit of the heavenward glance.

Not jeering or fearing,
sneering or smearing,
but cheering!
Peering upward, persevering!
Volunteering!
Eagerly revering
Your Nearing Appearing!

THE HEAD

But, speaking the truth in love, [we] may grow up in all things into Him who is the head—Christ—from whom the whole body, joined and knit together by what every joint supplies, according to the effective working by which every part does its share, causes growth of the body for the edifying of itself in love.

—Ephesians 4:15–16

JUST ABOVE YOUR SHOULDERS IS A THREE-POUND BLOB OF gray matter looking like a mushy cauliflower and containing billions of nerve cells arranged in intricate patterns designed to coordinate all your thoughts, feelings, behaviors, movements, and sensations. It's the supercomputer that runs your body. Anthropologist Henry Fairfield Osborn rightly observed: "To my mind, the human brain is the most marvelous and mysterious object in the whole universe."

Imagine the mayhem that would occur if your body rebelled against your brain, rejecting its thoughts and impulses. What if your bodily organs decided to function without synchronization from your head? What if your hands or feet or lungs had a mind of their own and refused to be governed by the brain's logical thoughts and automatic functions? We'd be quickly declared either insane or dead.

What makes a person think he can do anything of value apart from Christ who said, "Without Me you can do nothing" (John 15:5)? Such a person "has lost connection with the Head, from whom the whole body, supported and held together by its ligaments and sinews, grows as God causes it to grow" (Col. 2:19 NIV).

Christ is the Head (Eph. 4:15), the Head of every man (1 Cor. 11:3), the Head of the church (Eph. 5:23), the Head of the body (Col. 1:18), and the Head "of all principality and power" (Col. 2:10).

What your head is to the rest of your body, Jesus Christ is to His church. His body is made up of many various and strange parts, all perfectly designed and coordinated with infinite wisdom. Each part—whether tongue, tummy, or toe—has a vital purpose, and the brain harmonizes the whole.

In His church every member has a job to do. We're each custom-designed to fulfill a vital role in His kingdom. Every part is important. Yours may not appear a great role, but try functioning without your hands, your hip, or the hemoglobin of your blood. God has designed you for a special work, and His church is healthy only as each of us is instantly responsive to our living Head.

Is your place a small place?
Tend it with care; He set you there.
Is your place a large place?
Guard it with care! He set you there.
Whate'er your place, it is not yours alone, but his
Who set you there.

—JOHN OXENHAM, 1913

THE FIRSTBORN OVER ALL CREATION

He is the image of the invisible God, the firstborn over all creation.

—COLOSSIANS 1:15

MARK TWAIN ONCE WROTE, "WE HAD THE SKY, UP THERE, all speckled with stars, and we used to lay on our backs and look up at them, and discuss about whether they was made, or only just happened."

After years of telling us they "just happened," more and more scientists are now admitting that it appears "they was made." The whole world has been astounded at the incredible beauty transmitted back by the Hubble space telescope: multicolored arcs, distant spiraling galaxies, vibrant supernovas, and planetary rings. There are more stars in the heavens than there are grains of sand on the ocean floors.

The famous physicist Paul Davies wrote, "There is for me powerful evidence that there is something going on behind it all. . . . It seems as though somebody has fine-tuned nature's numbers to make the Universe. . . . The impression of design is overwhelming."[32]

Jesus did that! "For by Him all things were created that are in heaven and that are in earth, visible and invisible, whether thrones or dominions or principalities or powers. All things were created through Him and for Him" (Col. 1:16). In other words, He is the Firstborn—that is, the Heir—over all creation. He is, in fact, the Maker, the agent of the creation.

The book of Hebrews begins: "God, who at various times and in various ways spoke in time past to the fathers by the prophets, has in these last days spoken to us by His Son, whom He has appointed heir of all things, through whom also He made the worlds" (1:1–2).

So praise Him today! Sing the mighty power of God that made the mountains rise, that spread the flowing seas abroad and built the lofty skies. Sing the wisdom that ordained the sun to rule by day. The moon shines full at His command, and all the stars obey.

❦

Praise Him that He made the sun, day by day his course to run;
For His mercies still endure ever faithful, ever sure.
And the silver moon by night, shining with her gentle light;
For His mercies still endure ever faithful, ever sure.

—HENRY BAKER, MID-1800S

CHRIST WHO STRENGTHENS ME

I can do all things through Christ who strengthens me.

—PHILIPPIANS 4:13

ONE OF THE MOST REMARKABLE STORIES I'VE EVER READ IS the biography of Geoffrey Bull, a British missionary to Tibet who was captured and imprisoned by Chinese Communists. Geoffrey's captors stripped all his possessions from him, threw him in a series of prisons, robbed him of his Bible, and inflicted terrible suffering for three years. In addition to extreme temperatures and miserable physical conditions coupled with bodily abuse and near-starvation, Geoffrey was subjected to such mental and psychological torture that he feared he would go insane.

How did he keep his mind at peace? Though he had no Bible, he had studied the Bible all his life. So he began to go over the Scriptures systematically in his mind. He found it took him about six months to go all the way through the Bible mentally. He started at Genesis and recalled each incident and story as best he could, first concentrating on the content and then musing on certain points, seeking light in prayer.

He continued through the Old Testament, reconstructing the books and chapters to the best of his ability, then plunged into the New Testament and on to Revelation.

When he finished, he started over again. He later wrote, "The strength received through this meditation was, I believe, a vital factor in bringing me through, kept by the faith to the very end."[33]

Christ strengthens us, and He often does it in the weakness of our flesh and through the power of His Word. The Amplified Bible renders Philippians 4:13 in this way: "I have strength for all things in Christ Who empowers me [I am ready for anything and equal to anything through Him Who infuses inner strength into me; I am self-sufficient in Christ's sufficiency]."

We are self-sufficient in Christ's sufficiency. We are strong in the strength of His promises. We are bolstered by His Word, and our strength is renewed by waiting on Him.

Jesus! what a strength in weakness!
Let me hide myself in Him.
Tempted, tried, and sometimes failing,
He, my Strength, my victory wins.

—J. WILBER CHAPMAN, 1910

$\mathscr{A}$ SERVANT TO THE JEWS

For I tell you that Christ has become a servant of the Jews on behalf of God's truth, to confirm the promises made to the patriarchs.

— ROMANS 15:8 (NIV)

GOVERNOR EVAN BAHY OF INDIANA WAS ELECTED TO OFFICE at age thirty-four, making him the nation's youngest governor. Sometimes his youthfulness caused problems. When the Democratic National Committee met in Indianapolis in 1989, Governor Bahy held a reception at his official residence. He greeted each guest at the door with the words "Welcome to Indiana." The arriving dignitaries, taking him as a young staff member, gave him their coats and walked on to the reception. Slow to take offense, the governor gamely took their garments to the closet and hung them up.[34]

Though Jesus was King of the Jews, He took our coats and hung them up, living out His own words in Luke 22: "The kings of the Gentiles exercise lordship over them, and those who exercise authority over them are called 'benefactors.' But not so among you; on the contrary, he who is greatest among you, let him be as the younger, and he who governs as he who serves" (vv. 25–26).

Jesus served His people by living among them, healing their sick, soothing their hurts, raising their dead, feeding their poor, forgiving their sins. He didn't demand honor, though He didn't refuse it. He didn't require much, though He gave much. He was slain like a disgraced slave, yet over His head a sign announced: "King of the Jews."

No matter how rich and famous we become (or don't become), we're to consider ourselves slaves and to act as servants. What are the chances you'll encounter a small need you can meet in someone else's life today? Perhaps your spouse needs something as simple as a warm hug or a kind word. Perhaps your child or grandchild needs a note or phone call of encouragement. Perhaps a soul at work needs a random act of kindness.

"Be kindly affectionate to one another with brotherly love, in honor giving preference to one another; not lagging in diligence, fervent in spirit, serving" (Rom. 12:10–11).

The everlasting Son
Incarnate deigns to be;
Himself a servant's form puts on
To set His people free.

—Charles Coffin, 1736

IM

For this reason I also suffer these things; nevertheless I am not ashamed,
for I know whom I have believed and am persuaded that
He is able to keep what I have committed to Him until that Day.

—2 TIMOTHY 1:12

THE DEVOTIONAL WRITER SAMUEL D. GORDON KNEW A woman who had memorized much of the Bible, but old age began taking her memory from her. At last, she could only remember one verse of Scripture, 2 Timothy 1:12.

In time, she began to lose that verse, too, being able only to recall the words "what I have committed to Him." When she came to her deathbed, her loved ones noticed her lips moving. Bending low, they heard her repeating one solitary word over and over: "Him, Him, Him." Dr. Gordon noted that she had lost the whole Bible but one word. But in that one word, she had the whole Bible.

When we have Him, we have all we need: "He who did not spare His own Son, but delivered *Him* up for us all, how shall He not with *Him* also freely give us all things" (Romans 8:32, emphasis added). In Him is forgiveness of every sin, fellowship with Almighty God, and life forever and ever. In Him is love, joy, peace, and patience. We find strength in Him to bear our daily burdens, and stamina for our daily chores, and enthusiasm for our daily tasks. Our rest is in Him as well as our work.

In Him we find wisdom for life's dilemmas and guidance amid life's decisions. In Him we have an extended family, brothers and sisters with whom we'll spend eternity. All our emotional resources are in Him. We abide in Him, and He in us; and in Him we live and move and have our being.

There's no one like Him, no Friend like Him who sticks closer than a brother, and no Shepherd like Him who never leaves us nor forsakes us.

We have Him, He has us, and we are not ashamed. We glory in Him, for we know that He is able to keep what we have committed to Him until that day.

Are you rejoicing in Him today?

✦

Not what, but WHOM, I do believe,
That, in my darkest hour of need,
Hath comfort that no mortal creed
To mortal man may give;—
Not what, but WHOM!
For Christ is more than all the creeds,
And His full life of gentle deeds
Shall all the creeds outlive . . .
Not what, but WHOM!

—JOHN OXENHAM, 1913

HIM WHO FILLS ALL IN ALL

And He put all things under His feet, and gave Him to be head over all things to the church, which is His body, the fullness of Him who fills all in all.

—EPHESIANS 1:22–23

PETERSON'S PARAPHRASE RENDERS THE DESCRIPTIVE PHRASE "Him who fills all in all" this way: "He fills everything with his presence" (MESSAGE). The editors of the *Bible Knowledge Commentary* translate this: "the One who fills all things with all things [blessings]." William Hendrickson, one of my favorite commentators, says, "The words 'who fills all in all' means that Christ fills all the universe in all respects." It is a statement of Christ's omnipresence.

This means much to us on a personal level. One day a downcast woman recognized the famous Bible teacher F. B. Meyer on the train. They fell into conversation, and the woman shared with him her burden. For many years, she had cared for her crippled daughter. It was her mission and joy in life. She made tea for her each morning, then left for work, knowing that in the evening the daughter would greet her when she arrived home. When the daughter died, the mother was inconsolable. The house was unbearably empty, and home was no longer home.

Meyer offered a suggestion.

When you get home and put the key in the door, say aloud, "Jesus, I know You are here!" and be ready to greet Him directly when you open the door. And as you light the fire, tell Him what has happened during the day; if anybody has been kind, tell Him; if anybody has been unkind, tell Him, just as you would have told your daughter. At night, stretch out your hand in the darkness and say, "Jesus, I know You are here!"

Some time passed, and the two met again; but F. B. Meyer didn't recognize the woman at first. Her face radiated joy instead of gloom.

"I did as you told me," she said, "and it has made all the difference in my life, and now I feel I know Him."[35]

The French mystic, Brother Lawrence, called this "practicing the presence of God." Jesus Himself promised to never leave us or forsake us. He bids us draw near to Him Who Fills All in All.

Abide with me; fast falls the eventide;
The darkness deepens; Lord with me abide.
When other helpers fail and comforts flee,
Help of the helpless, O abide with me.

—HENRY F. LYTE, 1847

THE OVERSEER OF YOUR SOULS

For you were like sheep going astray, but have now returned
to the Shepherd and Overseer of your souls.

—1 PETER 2:25

THIS TITLE IS WHERE THE EPISCOPALIANS GET THEIR NAME. The Greek word for *overseer* is *episkopos*. The prefix *epi* can mean "upon" or "over." And from the stem word *skopos* we get our English word *scope*. It means "to oversee" or "to watch over." *Episkopos* refers to someone who watches over you for your good. In some of the older translations, this word is rendered "bishop."

It seems to me the word *overseer* conveys two ideas as it relates to Christ. The first is His *care* over us. He "oversees" the smallest details of my life, watching over me through the scope of His loving concern. As you read these words, you might be facing a painful situation, but your Overseer knows all about it. If He counts the hairs on your head, if He knows how many locusts filled the Egyptian sky, and how many birds were needed to feed Elijah, if He took the time to paint every rose in your garden, and if He counts the autumnal leaves on the trees and watches each fall to earth, then He surely knows the most minute detail of your concern. Nothing escapes His notice.

The second idea this word conveys is *control*. When I looked up the other fifteen times in which this word occurs in the Bible, this seemed the dominant idea. Genesis 39:4 says, "So Joseph found favor in [Potiphar's] sight, and served him. Then he made [Joseph] overseer of his house, and all that he had he put under his authority." Being the overseer of Potiphar's property meant that everything was under Joseph's control.

As my Overseer, Jesus not only cares for all the details of my life, He desires to control them for my good. All that I have is under His authority. Today, take your problems and potentials—your worship and your worries—and give them all to the Overseer of your soul. He is watching over you through the scope of His love, and He is able to bring all things under His authority.

Through the valley dark and deep,
He will comfort, He will keep,
I am safe in the tender Shepherd's care.

—ELIZA HEWITT, 1904

THE SHEPHERD

For you were like sheep going astray, but have now returned to the Shepherd and Overseer of your souls.

— 1 PETER 2:25

I'VE BEEN MULLING OVER THE NAMES AND TITLES OF CHRIST for a long time, but I thought of something today I hadn't previously considered: the names of God and of Christ in the Bible are all virtual promises. There's a sense in which these 150 names of Jesus represent 150 different promises. Take this familiar title, for example—Shepherd. Implied in that simple word is a promise: everything a shepherd was to his sheep, the Lord is to me. He leads me, feeds me, tends to my needs, and comforts me. He even bears me up in His arms as needed.

Several years ago, our church planned a citywide celebration that included a small petting zoo, and I promised to bring Trinka, our pet sheep. We had purchased Trinka as a lamb, bottle-feeding her until she was old enough for grain and grass. Now she was fat, fleecy, and heavy. But Trinka hated our station wagon and refused to go near its open tailgate.

I edged near her, stooped down, and spoke to her. Then I slipped my arms under her wooly belly, and both of us grunted as I lifted her from the ground, cradled her to my chest, and carried her to the car.

Halfway to the car, I suddenly thought of Deuteronomy 33:27: "The eternal God is your refuge, / And underneath are the everlasting arms." I had read that verse many times; I had visualized it as a pair of cupped hands holding people. But Moses, the writer of Deuteronomy, had been a shepherd on the backside of the desert. He understood sheep and had undoubtedly carried hundreds of them over difficult terrain and away from dangerous ravines. He had scooped up many an injured lamb.

Isaiah wrote, "He will feed His flock like a shepherd; / He will gather the lambs with His arm, / And carry them in His bosom" (Isa. 40:11). He also wrote, "Even to your old age, I am He, / And even to gray hairs I will carry you!" (Isa. 46:4).

Why do we struggle when we can snuggle safely in the Shepherd's everlasting arms? The eternal God is your Shepherd, "and underneath are the everlasting arms."

> *Let me hear Thy voice behind me,*
> *Calming all these wild alarms;*
> *Let me, underneath my weakness,*
> *Feel the everlasting arms.*

—CAROLINE L. SMITH, 1852

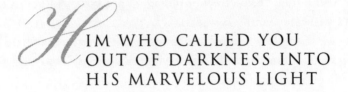

HIM WHO CALLED YOU OUT OF DARKNESS INTO HIS MARVELOUS LIGHT

But you are a chosen generation, a royal priesthood, a holy nation,
His own special people, that you may proclaim the praises
of Him who called you out of darkness into His marvelous light.

—1 PETER 2:9

CHRISTIANS ARE GIVEN HERE A FOURFOLD IDENTITY AND A single task. Our identity: we are "a chosen generation, a royal priesthood, a holy nation, [and] His own special people." Our task: to "proclaim the praises of Him who called us . . . into His marvelous light."

The process of reaching people with the light of Christ takes time. Perhaps you've been proclaiming His praises to your friends, coworkers, or family members, but so far there's little to show for it. Perhaps you're discouraged that they haven't yet found Christ.

It was seven years before William Carey, the Father of Missions, baptized his first convert in India. It was seven years before America's first missionary, Adoniram Judson, baptized his first convert in Burma. It was also seven years before Robert Morrison, the first Protestant missionary to China, saw his first Chinese convert.

Robert Moffat, the famous missionary to Africa, waited seven years to see the first evidence of the Holy Spirit's moving among the Bechuanas among whom he worked. Missionary Henry Richards worked seven years in the Congo before his first convert appeared at Banza Manteka.

The great writer and pastor of an earlier generation, A. J. Gordon, wrote,

It has seemed almost as though God had fixed this sacred biblical
number as the term of the missionary's apprenticeship, as I have found
it recurring again and again in the story of the planting of the

Gospel. . . . *"We are now seven years in this land,"* wrote Brother Batsch *of the Gossner Mission among the Kohls of India, "but through these long years it was but trial of our patience and endurance. . . . Everything seemed to be in vain, and many said the mission was useless. Then the Lord Himself kindled a fire before our eyes; and it seized not only single souls, but spread from village to village."*[36]

Keep proclaiming the praises of Him Who Called You Out of Darkness into His Marvelous Light. Your witness is not in vain.

⬥

To Father, Son, and Spirit,
All glory, praise and might,
Who called us out of darkness
To His own glorious light.

—GUILLAUME DE LA BRUNETIÈRE, SEVENTEENTH CENTURY

SHILOH

The scepter shall not depart from Judah,
Nor a lawgiver from between his feet,
Until Shiloh comes;
And to Him shall be the obedience of the people.

—GENESIS 49:10

I WOKE UP WORRIED TODAY, CONCERNED ABOUT A YOUNG person I love. A dull, gray sense of foreboding nagged at the corners of my mind. It was hard to shake off.

Anything worrying you today?

One of the earliest, but least known, names given to Jesus in the Bible is Shiloh, meaning "Peace." When Americans hear the word *Shiloh,* they think of the Civil War. Near the little town of Shiloh, Tennessee, on the banks of the Tennessee River, sixty-five thousand Northern troops battled forty-four thousand Confederate troops in the first major battle of the western front of the War Between the States. When it was over, twenty-four thousand men were killed, wounded, and missing.

What an ironic place for such a battle—the little Tennessee village named Peace.

In Genesis 49:10, this very word *Shiloh* was ascribed to the coming Messiah. It is one of the earliest predictions of Christ in the Bible. The old patriarch, Jacob, spoke this name as he dispensed his dying blessings upon his sons. Coming to his son Judah, Jacob's dim eyes managed to see into the future, and he announced that Judah would be the leading tribe among the Israelites and would remain so until the Messiah—Shiloh, the Man of Peace—came. The Man of Peace would be of the house and lineage of Judah.

The Living Bible simply puts it: "The scepter shall not depart from Judah until Shiloh comes, whom all people shall obey."

Sometimes we feel a civil war raging in our hearts or lives. Part of us wants to trust the Lord; part of us wants to collapse in worry. I find that sometimes part of me wants to obey, and the rest of me wants to yield to temptation.

Keep fighting on the right side, and Christ will win the victory. It may take a while to arrive at peace, but the Man of Peace—Shiloh—will prevail. He must win the battle.

Weep no more! Weep no more!
Zion, dry thy bitter tears!
Cast away all gloom and sadness,
For the Shiloh now appears.

—ANNA B. HOPPE, 1920

$\mathcal{T}$HE FRIEND WHO STICKS CLOSER THAN A BROTHER

A man who has friends must himself be friendly,
But there is a friend who sticks closer than a brother.

—Proverbs 18:24

This is the Bible's greatest verse on the subject of friendship, and it makes two transformational points.

First, to have friends we must be friendly. In other words, the secret to meaningful relationships is not found in seeking friends but in being a friend. When we're looking for friends, our own selfish needs drive the process: *I'm lonely. I need a friend. I wonder who can be my friend so that I'll not feel so sad and alone.* When we forget about our own needs and try to meet those of others, the process becomes Christlike. *He looks lonely today. She seems to have a lot of needs. What can I do to help that family and to be their friend?*

Ralph Waldo Emerson put it well when he wrote, "The only way to have a friend is to be one." Likewise, "You can make more friends in two months by becoming interested in other people than you can in two years by trying to get other people interested in you," wrote Dale Carnegie.[37]

The second part of Proverbs 18:24 describes an ultimate Friend for each of us, a Friend who is closer than a brother, a Friend who is truly interested in us with no thought of what's in it for Him. Somewhere there's someone who cares about us more than anyone else. There is someone who sees us and quietly interprets every line on our faces, every care in our hearts, every tear in our eyes.

In the Upper Room, Jesus said, "Greater love has no one than this, than to lay down one's life for his friends. You are my friends. . . . I have called you friends" (John 15:13–15).

If you're lonely today, you have a Friend Who Sticks Closer Than a Brother, and He's as near right now as He was to those twelve disciples.

What a Friend we have in Jesus, all our sins and griefs to bear!
What a privilege to carry everything to God in prayer!
O what peace we often forfeit, O what needless pain we bear,
All because we do not carry everything to God in prayer.

—JOSEPH M. SCRIVEN, 1855

THE FOURTH MAN

*"Look!" he answered. "I see four men loose, walking in
the midst of the fire; and they are not hurt, and the form
of the fourth is like the Son of God."*

—DANIEL 3:25

THIS WEEK I WAS VISITING WEST POINT MILITARY ACAD-
emy, where I dined one night in the mess hall with four thousand
cadets. It was a loud and boisterous meal, especially since it combined
supper with a pep rally designed to whip up support for the Army's
fledgling football team in preparation for its upcoming game against
the University of Connecticut.

Amid the noise and confusion, something attracted my attention.
A young cadet, without shame or embarrassment, quietly and deliberately bowed his head and spent a few moments thanking God for
his meal. When I approached him later in the evening, he told me he
was a Christian and he made no bones about it. "All the other cadets
know I'm a follower of Christ," he said.

In Daniel 3, three young men stood alone for God in the land of
Babylon, and when they refused to bow before Nebuchadnezzar's
image, they were condemned to death and thrown into a flaming furnace. But the preincarnate Christ joined them in the fire. What a
strange place to meet with Jesus, but the Fourth Man stepped from
the portals of glory into the fires of persecution; and it became a season of fellowship the three Hebrew children never forgot.

Charles Spurgeon once said,

*When [Jesus] in heaven heard them speak thus to King Nebuchad-
nezzar, He said, "Brave, brave men! I will leave the throne of God in
heaven to go and stand by their side"; and invisibly He descended, till
where the fires were glowing like one vast ruby, where the fierce
flame had slain the men that threw the three confessors into the burn-*

ing fiery furnace, He came and stood. And there they walked. It was the greatest walk that they had ever had. On those burning coals the four of them were walking together in sweet fellowship.

Never be afraid to stand up for Jesus. The Fourth Man will stand with you, imparting His strength and splendor.

Tried as by furnace fires, and yet
By God's grace only stronger made;
In future tasks before thee set
Thou shalt not lack the old-time aid.

—JOHN GREENLEAF WHITTIER, N.D.

THE COMMANDER OF THE ARMY OF THE LORD

Joshua went to Him and said to Him, "Are You for us or for our adversaries?" So He said, "No, but as Commander of the army of the LORD I have now come." And Joshua fell on his face to the earth and worshiped, and said to Him, "What does my Lord say to His servant?" Then the Commander of the LORD's army said to Joshua, "Take your sandal off your foot, for the place where you stand is holy."

—JOSHUA 5:13–15

WHAT A PHENOMENAL SCENE. AS THE ISRAELITES TENSELY prepared for the battle of Jericho, the Lord Jesus Himself—God the Son—sky-stepped from the throne of heaven onto the sands of the Negev for a last-minute summit meeting with the leader of Israel.

The Captain of the Army of the Lord represented, I believe, a preincarnate appearance of Christ. By that, I mean that Christ came to earth *in the form* of a human before He actually *became* a human at Bethlehem. It was Yeshua meeting Joshua.

We're given indications in the Bible that of the Trinity, the Father and the Holy Spirit remain invisible, but God the Son manifests God's presence to us. "No one has ever seen God, but God the One and Only [Son], who is at the Father's side, has made him known" (John 1:18 NIV).

On several occasions in the Old Testament, we glimpse the physical, literal appearance of God, a phenomenon some theologians call "Christophonies." The Christophany of Joshua 5, identified as the Commander of the Lord's Army, was designed to emphasize Christ's superiority over the military obstacles that lay ahead of the Israeli army. Joshua's ragtag forces, armed with swords and slingshots, were joined by an invisible angelic force who would win the victory. Hovering over the human armies of Joshua were the invisible armies of heaven, for the real battles are fought in heavenly places (Eph. 6:12).

We might have expected the Captain of the host to give military instructions or to impart some strategic insight. Instead the only message was: "Take off your shoes. The place where you are standing is holy." It isn't a matter of whether or not He's on our side; it's whether we are on His side. When we're aligned with Him, we're on holy ground. Our homes, offices, cars, or playing fields are holy places, for Christ is there, and with Him an innumerable company of angels.

We have friends in high places.

More than conquerors! There our Captain stands,
While our names are graven upon His hands;
Though the pow'rs of darkness against us frown,
We shall win the fight, and shall wear the crown.

—JEREMIAH RANKIN, NINETEENTH CENTURY

THE FOUNTAIN

In that day a fountain shall be opened for the house of David.

—ZECHARIAH 13:1

THE LATTER CHAPTERS OF ZECHARIAH PROVIDE FASCINATING information about the destiny of Israel during the final days of history. When Jesus appears at the moment of Armageddon, we're told, He will be like a free-flowing Fountain whose crimson streams will wash away the sins of Jewish people.

"There is a fountain opened," said Spurgeon in a great sermon on this text. "Not a cistern nor a reservoir, but a fountain. A fountain continues still to bubble up, and is as full after fifty years as at the first; and even so the provision and the mercy of God for the forgiveness and the justification of our souls continually flows and overflows."

This beautiful picture has inspired scores of our richest hymns, and it allows us to visualize Christ in a picturesque and perfect way—as our Fount of every blessing.

There is a fountain filled with blood drawn from Emmanuel's veins;
And sinners plunged beneath that flood lose all their guilty stains.

—WILLIAM COWPER, 1772

There's a fountain flowing from the Savior's side;
Life and health bestowing, since for us He died.
And the Word declareth, bathing there is free;
Who is he that dareth hinder you and me?

—OLD SWEDISH HYMN

Jesus, keep me near the cross,
There a precious fountain
Free to all, a healing stream
Flows from Calvary's mountain.

—FANNY CROSBY, 1869

The frustrating thing about time is that it always moves forward. There is no "R" on the stickshift, no reverse in the gears. Time never moves backward, not an inch, not a step, never. The hands of the clock always move clockwise, and the pages of the calendar are torn off in only one direction. Therefore a deed once done can never be undone. A word once spoken can never be unsaid. An opportunity missed can not be reclaimed in exactly the same way. As a result, all of us live with certain regrets.

When Satan comes to remind me of those regrets in my own life, I take a little visit to the Fountain. It's a soul-cleaning Fountain that pardons all our sins. When Jesus washes away our sins, they are gone for good; and we can forgive ourselves because we've been forgiven by Him who heals all wounds and expunges all records. You can feel clean today—totally clean, washed in the fountain filled with blood drawn from Emmanuel's veins.

Come where the fountain flows, river of life;
Healing for all thy woes, doubting, and strife.

—HENRY BURTON, 1878

THE SUN OF RIGHTEOUSNESS

But to you who fear My name
The Sun of Righteousness shall arise
With healing in His wings.

—MALACHI 4:2

HOW WONDERFULLY DOES THIS PASSAGE CLOSE THE PAGES OF Old Testament like the close of a weary, careworn day. But there's the anticipation of a predictable and spectacular sunrise on yonder side of night. In this last chapter of Malachi, we have the Old Testament's final promise of a coming Redeemer: Malachi compared Him to the sun. By and by, He will appear on the horizon of history with healing in His rays.

The sun—that golden orb—is the lord of light and the lamp of the day, the most magnificent visible object of the creation. Here is fullness of glory so intense we cannot look at it with direct eyesight. It sheds light and heat across the earth, bringing forth vegetation and herbs, drawing waters into vapors, sparking human energy, animating the cycles of nature, and providing warmth for life's existence. The rising of the sun is thoroughly constant, never missing its daily appointment in the eastern sky.

"The king of day is so vast and so bright that the human eye cannot bear to gaze upon him," said Spurgeon.

Jesus, like the sun, is the center and soul of all things, the fullness of all good, the lamp that lights us, the fire that warms us, the magnet that guides and controls us; He is the source and fountain of all life, beauty, fruitfulness, and strength; He is the fosterer of tender herbs of penitence, the quickener of the vital sap of grace, the ripener of fruits of holiness, and the life of everything that grows within the garden of the Lord. Whereas to adore the sun would be idolatry; it would be treason not to worship ardently the divine Sun of Righteousness.

As our world revolves around the sun, our souls must revolve around the Son. The gravity of His grace keeps us from wobbling into the dark voids of sin, and His healing rays give daily strength to our souls. Have you ever visualized Jesus like that? Ever thought of yourself as a planet, held in the grip of His gravity and warmed by the beams of His brilliance? He's the Sun of Righteousness, the Sun of our souls.

Hail the heav'nly Prince of Peace! Hail the Sun of Righteousness!
Light and life to all He brings, Ris'n with healing in His wings.
Mild He lays His glory by, Born that man no more may die.
Born to raise the sons of earth, Born to give them second birth.

—CHARLES WESLEY, 1739

MY COMPANION

"Awake, O sword, against My Shepherd,
Against the Man who is My Companion,"
Says the LORD of hosts.
"Strike the Shepherd, and the sheep will be scattered."

—ZECHARIAH 13:7

JESUS QUOTED THESE WORDS IN THE NEW TESTAMENT AS THE disciples fled the scene of our Lord's Passion. In Matthew 26:31, Jesus told the disciples in the upper room, "All of you will be made to stumble because of Me this night, for it is written, / 'I will strike the Shepherd, / And the sheep of the flock will be scattered.'"

This is therefore a messianic prediction.

Note that the Father uses the words "My Companion" to refer to the Son. The Hebrew word means "associate, neighbor, one in a close relationship, a relative." This speaks of the intimacy existing between the Father and the Son. Jesus later spoke of this throughout the Gospel of John as He continually referred to His special relationship with His Father.

This raises the mystery of the Trinity—how can there be one God who eternally exists in three persons? John Wesley once said, "Tell me how it is that in this room there are three candles and but one light, and I will explain to you the mode of the divine existence."

Christian philosopher Francis Schaeffer put it this way:

Often in a discussion someone will say, "Didn't God, then, if He is personal and if He loves, need an object for His love? Didn't He have to create? And therefore, isn't the universe just as necessary to Him as He is to the universe?" But the answer is, No. He did not have to create something face-to-face with Himself in order to love, because there already was the Trinity. God could create by a free act of the will because before creation there was the Father who loved the Son and there was also the Holy Spirit to love and be loved.[38]

One of the wondrous implications of the Trinity, then, is that God created you and me, not because He needed us for companionship's sake, for He already had a Companion. He made us because He freely wanted to. He doesn't *need,* but He greatly *desires,* your companionship today.

Holy, holy, holy! Lord God Almighty!
Early in the morning our song shall rise to Thee;
Holy, holy, holy, merciful and mighty!
God in three Persons, blessèd Trinity!

—REGINALD HEBER, 1826

HIS ANOINTED

The kings of the earth set themselves
And the rulers take counsel together,
Against the LORD and against His Anointed.

—PSALM 2:2

WORRIED ABOUT POLITICS? CURRENT EVENTS? WARS? ELECtions? Social trends? All our problems stem from humanity's continual state of rebellion against the Lord and against His Anointed One—Christ.

In what way is Christ the Anointed One? First, He was anointed with power at His baptism when the Holy Spirit descended on Him like a dove. When He preached in the synagogue of Nazareth shortly after His baptism, He said: "The Spirit of the LORD is upon Me, / Because He has anointed Me / To preach the gospel to the poor" (Luke 4:18).

At the end of His earthly ministry, Christ was anointed again— this time by Mary of Bethany, who "took a pound of very costly oil of spikenard, anointed the feet of Jesus, and wiped His feet with her hair" (John 12:3).

But Jesus *missed* a third anointing. Mark 16 tells us that on Easter Sunday a group of women came to the Lord's tomb bearing spices with which to anoint His body. He no longer had need for burial spices. He was alive!

In the future, according to Psalm 2, this Anointed One will be installed as King on Zion's holy hill (v. 6) and will receive the nations of the world as His inheritance (v. 8). He will resolve the intractable problems of humanity and bring the times and seasons to their preordained fulfillment. The horizons of history may seem deeply overcast today, but history is still His-story, and "blessed are all those who put their trust in Him" (v. 12).

I'm reading the headlines just like you; but I'm watching the horizon! Jesus is coming soon.

With restless and ungoverned rage
Why do the heathen storm?
Why in such rash attempts engage,
As they can ne'er perform?
The great in counsel and in might
Their various forces bring;
Against the Lord they all unite,
And His anointed King. . . .
But God, Who sits enthroned on high,
And sees how they combine,
Does their conspiring strength defy,
And mocks their vain design.

—NAHUM TATE AND NICHOLAS BRADY, 1698

THE HOLY ONE

But you denied the Holy One and the Just, and asked for
a murderer to be granted to you, and killed the Price of
Life, whom God raised from the dead.

—ACTS 3:14–15

PETER SPOKE THESE WORDS TO THE LEADERS OF JERUSALEM
only days after the ascension of Jesus Christ to heaven. He didn't coin
this title for Christ; it's an Old Testament messianic name, found in
Psalm 16:10: "You will not leave my soul in Sheol, / Nor will You
allow Your Holy One to see corruption."

The word *holy* means, in its original sense, "utterly different."
Christ is wholly unlike anyone else in history. He is matchless in His
claims about Himself, in His teachings, in His mission, in His dual
nature as the God-Man, in the purity of His life, in the redemptive
nature of His death, and in His resurrection from the grave. He is the
Different One, the perfect measure of holiness.

The reason we often feel okay about ourselves is because we're apt
to compare ourselves to others rather than to Christ, who is the imperial standard of holiness. This results in two opposite attitudes, both
of which, in the strange paradoxes of the soul, occur simultaneously.
On the one hand, we suffer feelings of inferiority, for everyone we
meet is better at something than we are. When we see someone making more money, reaching higher office, scoring more points, getting
better grades, or enjoying better health—well, we tend to feel envi-
ous and less valuable.

On the other hand, comparing ourselves with others gives us a low
marker for personal holiness, leading to unrealistic attitudes of superiority. The world is filled with terrorists, rapists, murderers, tramps,
cheats, and riffraff. But we're not like that. We do pretty well. We
even go to church.

On both levels, the measurements are flawed, for there is only one gauge of godliness. How do we stack up against the scorching purity and supreme holiness of Jesus Christ? He's the only barometer. The prophet Isaiah was smug in his own abilities till the day he saw the glory of God in the temple and heard the cry, "Holy, holy, holy is the LORD of Hosts." Falling on his face, he cried, "Woe is me, for I am undone!" (Isa. 6:3, 5).

Christ wants to work His holiness into our experience. He wants to sanctify, to perfect, to nurture, to implant His purity in our lives. It begins when we stop measuring ourselves with one another and cast our gaze to Him alone—the Holy One.

From the north to southern pole, Alleluia!
Let the mighty chorus roll, Alleluia!
"Holy, Holy, Holy One," Alleluia!
"Glory be to God alone!" Alleluia!

—STOPFORD BROOKE, 1881

THE JUST ONE

*They killed those who foretold the coming of the Just One,
of whom you now have become the betrayers and murderers.*

—Acts 7:52

ONE DAY A FAST-TALKING SALESMAN TRIED TO SELL HIS canned corn to a young grocer named Barney. The salesman was especially fond of the beautiful labels on his products. Barney, however, was not taken in. Reaching for one of the cans, he tore off the label, saying, "My customers don't eat labels. They eat what's inside."

At the back of the store was a small stove where Barney brewed tea. Opening the can, he heated the corn and found it tough and full of hulls. He sent the salesman packing, and word spread. Barney Kroger could be trusted, and his store became a great chain of supermarkets.[39]

Lots of people project a well-honed exterior. Clothes. Cars. Cash. Cocky smile. Confident persona. But what's on the inside is what God sees, and He cannot be fooled.

In his book *A Turtle on a Fencepost,* Allen C. Emery writes about his father,

> *Today I find myself still asking myself, "What would Daddy do?"
> when confronted with those decisions in business and in life that are
> so often not black and white, but gray. I am in debt to the memory-
> making efforts that my father made to imprint indelibly upon my
> mind the meaning of integrity.*
>
> *Once [my dad] lost a pair of fine German binoculars. He collected
> insurance only to find the binoculars a year later. Immediately he sent
> a check to the company and received a letter back stating that this sel-
> dom occurred and that they were encouraged. It was a small thing,
> but children never forget examples lived before them.*[40]

The Just One is a title for Christ that occurs twice in the Bible. Stephen used it in Acts 7 in a withering attack on the mob who had rejected Christ, and Paul used it in Acts 22:14 with the same general crowd. The Greek term in both places is *dikaios,* meaning "the righteous one, the upright one, the honest one, the pure one." It's the same word the Bible uses in telling *us* to be God's righteous people. As Thomas Watson once said, Christians are to be like their Master—"downright upright."

Will your children make decisions on integrity based on their memories of you?

I am resolved to go to the Savior,
Leaving my sin and strife;
He is the true One, He is the just One,
He hath the words of life.

—PALMER HARTSOUGH, 1896

THAT GREAT SHEPHERD OF THE SHEEP

May the God of peace who brought up our Lord Jesus from the dead, that great Shepherd of the sheep, through the blood of the everlasting covenant, make you complete in every good work.

—HEBREWS 13:20–21

WHEN I BEGAN PASTORING IN THE MOUNTAINS IN THE 1970s, I set aside time to study the subject of biblical shepherding. The word *pastor*, I knew, was translated from the Greek word for "shepherd." Even in English we see the correspondence between *pastor* and *pasture*. So I studied every word in the Bible relating to sheep and shepherds. In discovering what I was supposed to do as a pastor, I also learned what the Great Shepherd does for me. Biblical shepherds had six responsibilities:

1. *To love the flock.* The Hebrew words for *shepherd* and *friend* come from the same root. Alone on the remote hillsides, biblical shepherds became attached to their flocks. They assigned each sheep a name and spoke to each one daily. The sheep learned the shepherd's voice.

2. *To feed the flock.* Sheep need rich meadows of verdant grass, and the shepherd knows where to find them. In the same way, we need inner nourishment for our souls, and the Lord supplies the rich pasturage of His Word.

3. *To lead the flock.* Sheep aren't smart enough to know where to find still waters, so they rely on their shepherd to guide them. One of my favorite hymns says, "Savior, like a Shepherd lead me."

4. *To protect the flock.* Young David killed a lion and a bear that threatened his flock. Sheep are defenseless animals,

easily slaughtered by predators, needing constant watching. I have a ferocious enemy, too, and need constant protection.

5. *To tend the flock.* Sheep require attention. They need healing oil for cuts. They need worming and shearing. They sometimes break a leg or get mites in their ears. Like a sheep, I have many needs, but the Shepherd knows every one. We bring to Him our every care.

6. *To seek the lost.* Remember our Lord's story of the shepherd who left the ninety-nine in the fold to find the one who was straying? Jesus came to seek and to save those who are lost. This is what our Great Shepherd does for you and me.

This is what I'm supposed to be doing as pastor. I do it so poorly sometimes. Thank God Jesus does it perfectly and constantly. He is our Great Shepherd.

Savior, like a shepherd lead us, much we need Thy tender care;
In Thy pleasant pastures feed us, for our use Thy folds prepare.
Blessèd Jesus, blessèd Jesus! Thou hast bought us, Thine we are.

—Dorothy A. Thrupp, 1836

THE AUTHOR OF ETERNAL SALVATION

And having been perfected, He became the author of
eternal salvation to all who obey Him.

—HEBREWS 5:9

THE WORD *AUTHOR* OCCURS THREE TIMES IN THE BIBLE, always referring to the Lord Jesus. The word is *not* used of Him as the author and inspirer of Scripture, though He is that. All Scripture is breathed out by Him (2 Tim. 3:16), but that's not the actual implication of the threefold reference. So, then, what kind of "author" is He?

First, He's the Author of Eternal Salvation, the source of life eternal (Heb. 5:9). This gives us as believers a different slant on death from everyone else. My favorite Puritan writer, Thomas Watson, had this in mind when he wrote:

> *The world is but a great inn, where we are to stay a night or two, and be gone; what madness it is to set our heart upon our inn, as to forget our home. . . . We are travelers who take up our lodging here for a night; and Paul longed to be out of his inn. "I am in a strait betwixt two, having a desire to depart and to be with Christ; which is far better. . . ." The apostle did not say, "Having a desire to die," but "to depart." What a wicked man fears, a godly man hopes for. . . . Simeon, having taken Christ in his arms, cries out, "Lord, now lettest Thou Thy servant depart in peace" (Luke 2:29). He that hath taken Christ into the arms of his faith, will sing Simeon's song.*[41]

Second, Jesus is the Author of faith. Hebrews 12:2 says, "looking unto Jesus, the author and finisher of our faith." He's the source and center of our faith. He gives us the capacity for faith and has provided Himself as the object of faith. What's more, He's the perfecter of our faith. As we discover and appropriate His promises during trying times, we prove His trustworthiness.

Third, He's the Author of peace. Writing to the Corinthians, whose worship services were unorganized and bewildering to outsiders, Paul said, "God is not the author of confusion but of peace" (1 Cor. 14:33).

As I studied this, I thought of what Paul said in Ephesians 2:10: "We are His workmanship." The word *workmanship* is the Greek term *poiema*, from which we get our English word *poem*. It implies that God is a craftsman, an artist, a poet, an author. We are His masterpieces. Jesus begins His poems with faith, ends them with eternal salvation, and fills each stanza with peace.

Can you think of a better basis for healthy, godly self-esteem?

Author of life divine,
Who hast a table spread,
Furnished with mystic wine
And everlasting bread,
Preserve the life Thyself hast given,
And feed and train us up for Heav'n.

—JOHN WESLEY, 1746

THE VEIL

Therefore, brethren, having boldness to enter the Holiest by the blood of Jesus, by a new and living way which He consecrated for us, through the veil, that is, His flesh.

—HEBREWS 10:19–20

THE OLD TESTAMENT TABERNACLE WAS A TENT WITH TWO rooms separated by a thick, colorful curtain: the Holy Place and the Most Holy Place, also called the Holy of Holies. The Holy of Holies was the most special room in the world, containing the fabled ark of the covenant that represented, as it were, the footstool of God's throne.

The veil was woven of blue, purple, and scarlet yarn, with cherubim designed on it. It represented the body of Christ, the blue representing His heavenly origin, the purple His royalty, the scarlet His blood; and the cherubim symbolized the mighty angels guarding the heavenly Holy of Holies of which the most holy room in the tabernacle was a copy.

Only on the Day of Atonement could the high priest enter behind the veil to make atonement for the people and intercede before God on their behalf.

According to Matthew 27:51, at the very instant of our Lord's death, the temple veil ripped in two, top to bottom. God Himself took hold of the veil and rent it like a man tearing his clothes in grief.

He was signifying that now, through Jesus, we can enter the most special place in the universe: we can ascend into His presence. "Since we have confidence to enter the Most Holy Place by the blood of Jesus, by a new and living way opened for us through the curtain, that is, His body. . . . Let us draw near to God with a sincere heart in full assurance of faith" (Heb. 10:19-20, 22 NIV).

When I visualized this, it had a dramatic impact on my prayer life. Prayer is entering the gate of the tabernacle, passing the altar, marching across the courtyard, going past the laver, entering the tabernacle itself, moving through the first room with its furnishings, and entering boldly through the torn veil into the Holy of Holies to kneel at the very footstool of God's throne. We can do this with confidence, clothed in the righteousness of Christ. It's the greatest privilege we could ever imagine.

~~~

Earth hears, and trembling quakes
Around that tree of pain;
The rocks are rent; the graves are burst;
The veil is rent in twain.

—ANCIENT LATIN HYMN

</center>

THE AUTHOR AND FINISHER OF OUR FAITH

Looking unto Jesus, the author and finisher of our faith.

—HEBREWS 12:2

WHEN BUSINESSMAN ALLEN EMERY WAS IN THE WOOL BUSI-
ness, he once spent an evening with a shepherd on the Texas prairie.
During the night, the long wail of coyotes pierced the air. The shepherd's dogs growled and peered into the darkness.

The sheep, which had been sleeping, lumbered to their feet,
alarmed, bleating pitifully. The shepherd tossed more logs onto the
fire, and the flames shot up. In the glow, Allen looked out and saw
thousands of little lights. He realized those were reflections of the fire
in the eyes of the sheep. "In the midst of danger," he observed, "the
sheep were not looking out into the darkness but were keeping their
eyes set in the direction of their safety, looking toward the shepherd. I
couldn't help but think of Hebrews 12: 'looking unto Jesus, the author and finisher of our faith.' "[42]

This passage in Hebrews 12 immediately follows the roll call of the
heroes of the faith given in chapter 11. With that in mind, here's an
interesting explanation for the term "author of our faith" by Greek
scholar Kenneth S. Wuest:

> [The word "author"] is misleading and narrows the scope of the pas-
> sage. The word is made up of ago, "to lead," and arche, "the first."
> The compound word means "the chief leader, one that takes the lead
> in anything and furnishes the example." In our passage it describes
> Jesus as the One "who in the pre-eminence of His faith far surpasses
> the examples of faith commemorated in chapter 11."[43]

We have many great examples of faith in Hebrews 11, but if we
want to emulate their faith we shouldn't look to them but keep our
eyes on the greatest example of faith who ever existed: our Lord Jesus

Christ, "who for the joy that was set before Him endured the cross, despising the shame, and has sat down at the right hand of the throne of God" (Heb. 12:2). He is both our Model and our Mentor — the Author and Finisher (perfecter) of Our Faith.

When you hear coyotes, look to Him and live by faith, not by fretting.

Faith, mighty faith, the promise sees,
And looks to God alone;
Laughs at impossibilities,
And cries, "It shall be done!"

—CHARLES WESLEY, 1747

THE APOSTLE

Therefore, holy brethren, partakers of the heavenly calling,
consider the Apostle and High Priest of our confession, Christ Jesus.

— HEBREWS 3:1

WHEN JESUS CALLED HIS TWELVE FOLLOWERS BY THE SEA OF Galilee, He dubbed them *disciples;* but He soon promoted them to *apostles*. What's the difference? The word *disciple* means "learner." It refers to someone who follows, learns, and seeks to emulate the teacher. The word *apostle* comes from the Greek word *apostolos,* which means "to be sent, to go."

The word *apostle* is used three ways in the Bible. In a restricted sense, it refers to those twelve original followers of Christ who came to Him, learned from Him, and were sent forth from Him to establish His church.

In a broader sense, the word *apostle* refers to all those whom Christ sends out. In Acts 14:14, for example, Barnabas was called an apostle, though he was not one of the original Twelve. Galatians 1:19 called James, the Lord's brother, an apostle. Others included Silvanus and Timothy (1 Thess 1:1, 2:6); Apollos (1 Cor. 4:6, 9); Titus (2 Cor. 8:23); and Epaphroditus (Phil. 2:25). Interestingly, the word *missionary* is a Latin-based word with exactly the same meaning as the Greek-rooted word *apostle*. The stem of both words means "to be sent."

The third use of this word in the Bible is as a title for Jesus Christ. He was the Sent One, God's missionary from heaven to earth, the ultimate Apostle. The Gospel of John makes this clearer than any other book in the Bible, for the word *sent* occurs there fifty-seven times, including the following:

    I have not come of Myself, but He who sent Me is true. (7:28)

    I am from Him, and He sent Me. (7:29)

                His Names in Hebrews

—∽ *He who sent Me is true. (8:26)*

—∽ *He who sent Me is with Me. (8:29)*

—∽ *I must work the works of Him who sent Me. (9:4)*

Jesus is God's personal missionary to you. He wants to make you His disciple that He might use you as His apostle. We might say there are three stages in the Christian experience. We are His pagans to be evangelized, for He is our missionary. We are His pupils to be taught, for we are His disciples. We are His preachers being sent, for He said, "As the Father has sent Me, I also send you" (John 20:21).

At which stage are you?

Over mountain, plain or sea,
Here am I, send me!
I'll go to the ends of the earth for Thee,
Here am I, send me!

—J. GILCHRIST LAWSON, C. 1910

IM WHO ENDURED SUCH HOSTILITY

For consider Him who endured such hostility from sinners against Himself, lest you become weary and discouraged in your souls.

—HEBREWS 12:3

AFTER NEARLY THIRTY YEARS IN THE MINISTRY—TWENTY-five of them pastoring the same church—I know the withering virulence of discouragement. Someone has called discouragement "the occupational hazard of ministry." I've had a few bouts with this hooligan myself, and on a few occasions I've been about as low as the underside of a rock in the bottomlands.

I once asked the preaching legend W. A. Criswell if he had suffered discouragement during his fifty years as pastor of the First Baptist Church of Dallas. He grinned and exploded with his customary fervor: "World without end, lad!"

"Well," I asked, "what did you do?"

"I just let it pass," he said. "I found that discouragement doesn't usually reside in the circumstances. It's almost always in my own heart and head. I just have to get back to seeing things as God does. He's never discouraged. He is incapable of discouragement."

The writer of Hebrews was writing to Jewish Christians who were losing heart because of renewed persecution. They were facing ridicule and rejection, loss of property and opportunity, and perhaps even imprisonment and death—all because of their adherence to Christianity.

The way to renew strength and revive courage, the writer said, is to "consider" Jesus. Think about Him. Focus on Him. See Him. Ponder Him. Picture Him in your mind's eye. Study Him afresh. "Consider Him who endured such hostility against Himself, lest you become weary and discouraged in your souls."

Missionary Amy Carmichael once said, "There is no provision in the whole Bible for a despondent Christian."[44] Or as Moses put it in Deuteronomy 1:21: "The LORD God of your fathers has spoken to you; do not fear or be discouraged."

John Bunyan, the tinker of Bedford, England, was imprisoned for years because of his faith in Christ, separated by bars from his wife and children, including his little blind daughter, Mary. He struggled with disheartening circumstances, but he "considered" Jesus and kept his eyes on the Author and Finisher of his faith. As a result, the books flowing from his pen in Bedford Jail made the unlettered Bunyan one of the greatest Christian preachers and leaders of all time. Bunyan's philosophy is summed up in a little poem he wrote, as recorded in his classic *Pilgrim's Progress*:

He who would valiant be 'gainst all disaster,
Let him in constancy follow the Master.
There's no discouragement shall make him once relent
His first avowed intent to be a pilgrim.

—MODIFIED IN VERSE FORM BY PERCY DEARMER, 1906

$\mathcal{H}$E WHO MADE ME WELL

He who made me well said to me, "Take up your bed and walk."

—JOHN 5:11

JOHN 5 TELLS THE STORY OF A MAN WHO HAD BEEN PARA-
lyzed for thirty-eight years. Day after day, he was placed at the pool of
Bethesda in Jerusalem, for there was a tradition that an angel periodi-
cally stirred up the waters. The first person to jump into the pool was
healed; so a great number of sick lingered around the pool, waiting
for the churning of the waters. For this reason, the pool of Bethesda
became a sort of hospital in those days. On that day, Jesus was making
a hospital visit.

This picture is easy for me to visualize for several reasons. First, as
a pastor I've made countless hospital visits for thirty years. Second,
my wife is growing increasingly paralyzed from multiple sclerosis, so
we can identify with this man. Perhaps MS was the very disease he
battled. Third, I've been to Jerusalem and visited this actual location.
Excavations have shown it had five uncovered colonnades, just as
John described it (v. 2).

The interesting thing about this story is that the man seemed to
have no knowledge of who Jesus was at the time of his healing, and
little appreciation afterward. After his healing, the authorities asked
him, "Why are you carrying your bed mat on the Sabbath?" The
man's only response was: "He who made me well said to me, 'Take up
your bed and walk.'"

Later Jesus found the man in the temple and reminded him, "See,
you have been made well. Sin no more, lest a worse thing come upon
you" (v. 14). The man immediately told the authorities it was Jesus of
Nazareth who had healed him. The man's attitude explains why
Jesus warned Him, "Stop sinning, lest a worse thing come upon you."

Is there something worse than lying paralyzed for thirty-eight
years? Yes. Hell and eternal damnation.

How foolish the man was, to accept the healing without reverencing the Healer and to receive the blessings without living a life of faith and obedience. Jesus will one day heal all His children of every disease of body, mind, and soul. Throughout eternity we will refer to Christ as "He Who Made Me Well."

Let's begin now reverencing the Healer and living a life of trust, obedience, and praise.

Jesus only, Jesus ever,
Jesus all in all we sing,
Savior, Sanctifier, and Healer,
Glorious Lord and coming King.

—A. B. SIMPSON, 1890

THE CARPENTER

Is this not the carpenter?

—MARK 6:3

WHY A CARPENTER? EVERY ASPECT OF THE EARTHLY LIFE OF Christ was preplanned, preordained, and predestined. He could have come as a king, a shepherd, a rabbi, a priest, or a physician. All would have been appropriate. But a carpenter? So far as I've seen, there's nothing in the Old Testament that predicted this. The prophets announced in advance every other aspect of Jesus' life. Why, then, was He raised in a carpenter's house, and why did He become a carpenter? Assuming Jesus started His trade about age thirteen, He spent many more years building houses than preaching sermons. Some reasons:

First, He came to build a ladder to heaven, and it required hammers, nails, and wood. The very implements Jesus knew so well were the ones He utilized at Calvary for building an entranceway for us into eternity.

Second, He came to build a temple in three days. When His enemies demanded a sign, He replied, "Destroy this temple, and in three days I will raise it up." They said, "'It has taken forty-six years to build this temple, and will You raise it up in three days?' But He was speaking of the temple of His body" (John 2:19–21).

Third, Jesus came to build His church (Matt. 16:18). Buildings are not churches, though churches often meet in buildings. The church is the people—living stones being built into a holy habitation for our Lord.

Fourth, Jesus came to build us. We're His construction project. Paul wrote in 1 Corinthians 3:9: "You are God's building." The Lord Jesus wants to build us up in faith, in love, in maturity, and as a glorious monument of His grace.

Fifth, He's building a home for us "over yonder." He has gone to prepare a place for us in the city whose builder and maker is God.

Visualize Him today, wearing His workman's apron, wielding hammers and nails, busy on your behalf—the Carpenter of Nazareth. He can straighten bent nails, sand rough surfaces, clean dirty timbers, and make a beautiful temple of your life. He who has begun "a good work in you will carry it on to completion" (Phil. 1:6 NIV).

⌇

O Carpenter of Nazareth, Builder of life divine,
Who shapest man to God's own law, Thyself the fair design,
Build us a tower of Christlike height, that we the land may view,
And see, like Thee, our noblest work, our Father's work to do.

—JAY T. STOCKING, 1912

A PROPHET WITHOUT HONOR

*So they were offended at Him. But Jesus said to them,
"A prophet is not without honor except in his own country
and in his own house." Now He did not do many mighty works there
because of their unbelief.*

—MATTHEW 13:57–58

HE WROTE THE STORIES OUR CHILDREN LOVE: "THE UGLY Duckling," "The Little Mermaid," "The Princess and the Pea," and "The Emperor's New Clothes." Hans Christian Andersen, spinner of fairy tales, was born in the slums of Odense, Denmark, to a shoemaker and a washerwoman. At age fourteen, he set off for Copenhagen where he slowly built his career.

In 1843, Paris received Anderson like a hero and he hobnobbed with the most famous authors and artists of his day. But while there, he learned that his drama, "Agnete and the Merman," had been booed after its first performance back in Copenhagen. This was his reaction:

I wish my eyes may never again see the home which can only see my shortcomings but fails to realize what great gifts God has given me! I hate those who hate me; I curse those who curse me . . . ! They spit on me, they trample me to the mud, and yet I am a poet of a kind God did not give them many of—and in my dying hour I shall ask God never to give any such to that nation again. . . . Here, in this large foreign city, the best known and the noblest among the spirits of Europe receive me with kindness and love, meet me as a kindred soul, and at home the boys are spitting at the best creation of my heart. . . . I wish I had never seen that place, I wish the eternal God will never again let anybody with a name like mine be born there; I hate the home, just as it hates and spits on me.[45]

Jesus suffered a much deeper hometown rejection, deeper than any other man's; but He uttered no words of hatred, hurt, anger, and angst. He simply went His way, determined to die for them anyway. He wasn't embittered; He was simply a Prophet Without Honor. "He came unto his own, and his own received him not. But as many as received him, to them gave he power to become the sons of God, even to them that believe on his name" (John 1:11–12 KJV).

Ever feel a pang of rejection from family or friends? Take heart! You're in good company. Keep your eyes on Him and forge ahead!

Without honor, without hatred,
Though rejected was He,
Without ranting, without rancor,
He died on the Tree.
He died there for me.

THE BRIDEGROOM

Behold, the bridegroom is coming.

—MATTHEW 25:6

DR. THOMAS LAMBIE, VETERAN MISSIONARY TO AFRICA, TOLD of a widower who, wanting to find a groom from his daughter, invited all the noblemen in the country to come for a week of entertainment at his castle. Early on the day of their arrival, a knocking was heard at the back gate, and an apparently deformed man on crutches appeared. Members of the house staff threw a few crusts to him, then slammed the gate in his face. But the tramp continued beating on the oaken panel with his crutches.

"Isn't this the day for guests to seek the nobleman's daughter?" he cried. Peals of laughter echoed as cooks, servants, and soldiers gathered to mock the poor fool. The daughter, hearing the noise, went to inquire. "What is it you want?" she asked the beggar.

"I have seen you while I myself was unnoticed, and I love you and have come to ask for your hand in marriage." After a moment's quiet reflection, the daughter replied, "Yes, I will marry you."

"I will be back in a year and a day," said the beggar, turning and limping away. A pall descended over the castle. The friends left in anger. The nobleman alternately lectured and begged his daughter to come to her senses, but she only smiled gently.

A year passed, then another day. At high noon, music was heard, and the sun flashed on polished armor. A courier spurred to the gate with astonishing news: the king's son was approaching. The nobleman and his daughter barely reached the castle gate in time. There, riding between rows of knights, was the royal prince mounted on a white charger and clad in golden armor. "My love," he said, "I have come back for you as I promised."

Her eyes filled with tears as she replied, "I knew you'd come." So he took his bride to his royal palace. But before she left there was time for one of the maids to ask, "How did you know the beggar was the prince in disguise?"

"Ah," she said, "I looked into his eyes and saw something there. I listened to his voice and something I heard there made me know that he was indeed the son of the king."[46]

It is like that. The Lord Jesus came in humility as the poorest of men, but soon He will return in splendor for His Bride, the church. The Bible says, "Behold, the bridegroom is coming."

Behold the Bridegroom cometh!
And all may enter in
Whose lamps are trimmed and burning
Whose robes are white and clean.

—GEORGE ROOT, 1894

FISHER OF MEN

Then He said to them, "Follow Me, and I will make you fishers of men." They immediately left their nets and followed Him.

—MATTHEW 4:19–20

IN LUKE'S VERSION OF THIS STORY, WE LEARN THAT JESUS told Peter, "Do not be afraid. From now on you will catch men" (5:10). The Greek word Luke used was *zōgreō*, which literally means "to take alive." This word occurs in only one other place in the Greek New Testament, in 2 Timothy 2:25–26, which says: "[Correct] those who are in opposition, if God perhaps will grant them repentance, so that they may know the truth, and that they may come to their senses and escape the snare of the devil, having been taken captive by him to do his will."

In the first instance, Jesus was fishing for men, wanting to take them alive. But there's another fisherman trolling the ocean of humanity. The devil is fishing for the souls of men, women, boys, and girls, wanting to take them alive. In both cases, the same word is used, but with drastically different outcomes.

In Matthew 4:19–20, the term "fishers of men" describes not Jesus, but His followers. It's obvious, however, that Jesus is the ultimate Fisher of Men, and that He longs to recruit us into His fleet.

Put another way, personal evangelism is our *responsibility*. That is, it is our *response* to His *ability*. Our response is to obey the command: "Follow Me." His ability is the attached promise: "I will make you fishers of men."

William Evans, in an old book on soul-winning, wrote,

It is not enough to be evangelical. We must be evangelistic. The evangelical *church is a reservoir of pure water without a pipe running anywhere. If you will take the trouble to go to it and climb the embankment, you will get a good drink. The* evangelistic *church is a reservoir of pure water with a pipe running to every heart in the com-munity, and every nation in the world.*[47]

It isn't always easy to share our faith with another person, but if we're really following Jesus we'll really be fishing for souls. The Lord will empower us to take people alive. Even though I'm somewhat shy and retiring, I go out each week with a team from my church seeking to share the gospel with prospects. It hasn't been easy, but it's been worth it whenever we've found someone ripe and ready for the gospel. I'm sure that in heaven I'll wish I had done more of it.

After all, it's our response-ability.

~~~

Rescue the perishing, care for the dying,
Snatch them in pity from sin and the grave;
Weep o'er the erring one, lift up the fallen,
Tell them of Jesus, the mighty to save.

—FANNY CROSBY, 1869

GHOST

When the disciples saw Him walking on the sea, they were troubled, saying, "It is a ghost!" And they cried out for fear. But immediately Jesus spoke to them, saying, "Be of good cheer! It is I; do not be afraid."

—MATTHEW 14:26–27

A COUPLE OF YEARS AGO, I PREACHED A SERIES OF SERMONS entitled, "Hurry Up, Lord!" about the delays of Christ in the Gospels. This is one of them. After a busy day of ministry, Jesus hurried the disciples into a boat while He Himself climbed a mountainside to pray. The disciples rowed into a squall. The wind opposed them, the sea was rough, and they struggled at the oars. "In the fourth watch of the night, Jesus went to them, walking on the sea" (v. 25). The fourth watch extended from 3 AM to 6 AM.

Jesus could have rescued them at nine o'clock, and by ten they'd have been safely tucked into warm beds. Why make them struggle all night? Why doesn't God more quickly rescue us from uncomfortable settings? Why doesn't He instantly answer our prayers and solve our problems? I don't know all His reasons, but I do know these three things:

1. *When they couldn't see Him, He could see them.* Mark's account says, "Then He saw them straining at rowing, for the wind was against them" (Mark 6:48). All they could see from their perspective was the dark façade of the mountains against an even blacker sky. But from His perch on the mountain, Jesus could see their little boat, a speck on the lake, and He knew their struggles. When we think Jesus has forgotten about us, He is watching closely.

2. *When they didn't know it, Jesus was praying for them.* He had gone to the mountain to pray, and He was undoubtedly praying for His friends on the lake. The books of Romans

and Hebrews tell us that Jesus is now at the right hand of God, making intercession for us. He prays to His Father about our needs.

3. *When we can't go to Him, He comes to us.* At the right time from His perspective, Jesus hastened down the hillside, stepped onto the blue liquid of Galilee, and walked across the waves to His friends. They thought He was a ghost, but He climbed into the boat with them, and all was well.

If you're wondering why God isn't answering your prayers as quickly as you'd like, take heart. When you can't see Him, He's watching you. When you don't know it, He is praying for you. And when you can't come to Him, He comes to you in His perfect timing.

His wisdom is sublime,
His heart profoundly kind;
God never is before His time,
And never is behind.

—J. J. Lynch, N.D.[48]

A HEN

O Jerusalem, Jerusalem, the one who kills the prophets and stones those who are sent to her! How often I wanted to gather your children together, as a hen gathers her chicks under her wings, but you were not willing!

—MATTHEW 23:37

I HAVE CHILDHOOD RECOLLECTIONS OF VISITING MY GRAND-parents at their farmhouse atop a hill on the Tennessee/North Carolina border. They raised chickens, and I was always delighted when the mother hen strutted around with her brood of little ones, clucking in pride. But if my little dog, Tippy, growled at them, the old hen instantly plopped down and ruffled out her feathers. All her little chicks scrambled beneath her wings for safety. She fluffed out to twice her normal size, her hatchlings well hidden and unafraid.

If God the Father is pictured as an eagle in the Bible (Exod. 19:4), and if God the Spirit is likened to a dove (Matt. 3:16), our Lord Jesus is like a mother Hen in whom we can find refuge, warmth, safety, and security amidst the growling threats of our adversary and our adversities.

This is simply the continuation of an Old Testament portrait of God's care. In Psalm 17, when the shepherd David was distressed by opponents on every side, he prayed, "Hide me under the shadow of Your wings, / From the wicked who oppress me, / From my deadly enemies who surround me" (vv. 8–9). When he was fleeing from the armies of Saul in Psalm 57, he prayed, "O God, be merciful to me! / For my soul trusts in You; / And in the shadow of Your wings I will make my refuge, / Until these calamities have passed by" (v. 1).

Psalm 91 contains a precious promise for believers in times of calamity: "He shall cover you with His feathers, / And under His wings you shall take refuge" (v. 4).

In the middle of the twentieth century, when Communism was

trapping Eastern Europe behind an Iron Curtain and mainland China behind a Bamboo Curtain, the missionaries of the China Inland Mission, finding themselves in great danger, coined a new phrase to comfort themselves. They said they were abiding under the "Feather Curtain" of God.

How often, when I've been too tired to pray and too worried to sleep, have I gone to His Word, found a promise, reminded myself of my safety in Him, and scrambled under the Feather Curtain of my Lord Jesus. Go ahead and picture it in your minds. It's all right. It's biblical. Jesus is like a mother Hen, and under his wings we safely abide, come what may. Our lives are "hidden with Christ in God" (Col. 3:3).

Under His wings, under His wings,
Who from His love can sever?
Under His wings my soul shall abide,
Safely abide forever.

—WILLIAM O. CUSHING, C. 1896

A THIEF IN THE NIGHT

Watch therefore, for you do not know what hour your Lord is coming. But know this, that if the master of the house had known what hour the thief would come, he would have watched and not allowed his house to be broken into. Therefore you also be ready; for the Son of Man is coming in an hour you do not expect.

—MATTHEW 24:42–44

ONCE AND ONLY ONCE HAVE I DREAMED OF THIS. IT WAS AN overcast day and I saw myself inside a house, standing near a window. Glancing outside, I noticed the clouds were picking up speed as they drifted across the sky. As their velocity increased, they began swirling around in the sky like a gathering whirlwind, and I began to feel a tug, then a powerful vacuum. The heavens suddenly broke open and a brightness shone through. I was swept upward like a particle of steel drawn to a magnetic force, off my feet and into the air. Realizing what was happening, I thought, *He's back!* But almost instantly in my dream, I felt a sense of panic as I urgently looked from side to side, seeking a dear one who wasn't ready for the coming of the Thief in the Night.

Jesus warned that His return would be sudden and swift. Paul, quoting our Lord, told the Thessalonians,

But concerning the times and the seasons, brethren, you have no need that I should write to you. For you yourselves know perfectly that the day of the Lord so comes as a thief in the night. For when they say, "Peace and safety!" then sudden destruction comes upon them, as labor pains upon a pregnant woman. And they shall not escape. But you, brethren, are not in darkness, so that this Day should overtake you as a thief. . . . Therefore, let us not sleep, as others do, but let us watch and be sober. (1 Thessalonians 5:1-4, 6)

How do you prepare for the imminent return of Christ?

- ✦ *Admit that you are separated from God by your sin and moral failure. The Bible teaches that all have sinned and have fallen short of God's standards (Rom. 3:23).*

- ✦ *Acknowledge that Jesus Christ died for your sins and rose from the grave. According to Romans 10:9, if we confess with our mouths Jesus as Lord and believe in our hearts that God has raised Him from the dead, we shall be saved.*

- ✦ *Ask Him by faith to come into your life, forgive your sin, and become your Savior. "Whoever calls on the name of the LORD shall be saved," says Romans 10:13.*

For those who know Him, He will come not as a Thief in the Night but as Lord of the Light. Watch, therefore, and be ready.

It may be any day now.

In an hour to us unknown, as a thief in deepest night,
Christ shall suddenly come down, with all His saints in light.

—CHARLES WESLEY, 1742

THE CHRIST

"Who do you say that I am?"
Peter answered and said to Him, "You are the Christ."

—MARK 8:29

CHRIST IS A TITLE RATHER THAN A NAME, THE GREEK FORM
of the Hebrew *Messiah*—literally "Anointed One."

The concept of anointing first appears in Scripture in Genesis 28,
when Jacob slept with a stone for his pillow. During the night, he
dreamed of a staircase reaching to heaven on which the angels of God
were ascending and descending. It was a God-given vision of the
coming Messiah, the gateway to heaven (see John 1:51).

"Early the next morning Jacob took the stone he had placed under
his head and set it up as a pillar and poured oil on top of it. He called
that place Bethel" (Gen. 28:18 NIV). This is the first occurrence of an
oil anointing in God's Word.

Later Moses used oil to anoint Aaron as high priest, Samuel
anointed David to be king, and Elijah anointed Elisha as a prophet of
God. The act of anointing with oil was what people used to set apart
the special roles of prophet, priest, and king in Hebrew society. It was
emblematic of the Holy Spirit being poured upon these people.

But the Old Testament taught something more: a Messiah would
come who would be anointed with unlimited power, with an unlimited measure of the Holy Spirit, with unlimited glory. This person
would receive an ultimate, inexhaustible, everlasting anointing. He
would be the definitive and eternal "Anointed One." Messiah. Christ.

At Jesus' baptism, the Holy Spirit descended on our Lord like a
dove, signifying His being anointed as the eternally definitive
Prophet, Priest, and King, capable of bearing all our burdens, enrich-
ing all our days, and imparting life abundant and eternal to all His
children. This is the Christ, *our* Anointed One.

Christ is the world's Redeemer,
The lover of the pure,
The Fount of heavenly wisdom,
Our trust and hope secure;
The Armor of His soldiers,
The Lord of earth and sky;
Our Health while we are living,
Our Life when we shall die.

—COLUMBA, SIXTH CENTURY

THE CHRIST OF GOD

He said to them, "But who do you say that I am?"
Peter answered and said, "The Christ of God."

—LUKE 9:20

WHEN DR. ARTHUR WAY WAS TRANSLATING THE LETTERS OF Paul from Greek into English, he avoided using the title *Christ*. Instead, when he came to the Greek word *Christos*, he rendered it as "Messiah" in his version of the Bible. "It tends to bring the modern reader nearer to the attitude of the ancient," he explained.

Dr. Way had a way with words. The terms *Messiah* and *Christ* are one and the same, the former coming from the Hebrew and the latter coming from the Greek. It was our Lord's official designation, and it occurs 571 times in the New Testament. It became the name by which our Lord's followers were identified: Christ-ians, or Christ-ones. But Luke 9:20 is the Bible's only reference to Him as "The *Christos* of God." The Swiss scholar, F. L. Godet, suggests that the phrase implies that He (Christ) belonged to God, as in *Son of God, Lamb of God,* or *Servant of God*.

He was the Messiah of God on our behalf.

I feel sorry for people who don't realize this. The great American author Gertrude Stein, battling the despair of an empty life philosophy, wrote tersely, "There ain't no answer. There ain't going to be an answer. There never has been an answer. That's the answer."[49]

But there *is* an answer to the riddle of life, and it's a good one. There's an answer to your purpose and reason for existence. There's an answer to your problems. There's an answer to your deepest fears and most painful failures. There's an answer to your mood today.

It's the Christ of God. He's just as alive and alert as He was when standing with Peter in the northern slopes of Israel. You can talk to Him just as naturally as talking to a friend. God sent Him for you, and you have His full attention.

I bless the Christ of God, I rest on love divine,
And with unfaltering lip and heart, I call the Savior mine.
His cross dispels each doubt; I bury in His tomb
Each thought of unbelief and fear,
Each lingering shade of gloom.

—Horatius Bonar, 1861

GOOD TEACHER

Now as He was going out on the road, one came running, knelt before Him, and asked Him, "Good Teacher, what shall I do that I may inherit eternal life?" So Jesus said to him, "Why do you call Me good? No one is good but One, that is, God."

—MARK 10:17–18

ONLY ONE PERSON IN THE BIBLE EVER ADDRESSED JESUS LIKE this: the rich young ruler. Our Lord's enigmatic response is puzzling, for He seemed to reject the name. "Why do you call Me good?" He said. "No one is good but . . . God."

We know Jesus was, in fact, good; we know He was God. Why then did He deflect the young man's compliment? Some say, "Well, Jesus was admitting He was neither good nor God." But we must read this more carefully. Jesus didn't deny being good, and He didn't deny being God. He just asked the young man if he really understood the implications of what he was saying.

Jesus said, in effect, "'Good Teacher' is an odd thing to call Me. Don't you realize only God is good? In calling Me good you are really calling Me God. Are you willing to live with the implications of that? Are you willing to obey Me in what I'm about to tell you? If so, then give away your possessions, take up your cross, and follow Me."

If that seems harsh to you, consider the timing of the story. It didn't happen in the early days of Christ's ministry or alongside the Sea of Galilee during those refreshing years of rural labor. Jesus was making His final approach to Jerusalem, and the shadow of the cross fell heavily on His pathway. This incident occurred as He was leaving for Jericho, Bethany, Jerusalem, and Calvary. His followers were about to be torn inside out. The next weeks would be ones of testing, terror, and tragedy. Satan was going to exploit every chink in their armor, every spot of idolatry in their hearts.

Jesus was telling the young man, "If you're going to follow Me, it's going to turn your life inside out and upside down, and your money is a luxury you can't afford. You're going to be tested. And after the resurrection, you'll be persecuted and flung to the ends of the earth as My ambassador. Go ahead and start detaching, start divesting, start getting ready now."

But the young man couldn't discern the times. He didn't realize how urgent and transient the moment was.

Do we? We do only as we acknowledge Him as our Good Teacher.

Good Teacher, I know You are good, You are God;
You wended your way to Calvary's sod.
Be Lord of my life and Master of all,
And make me responsive to Your beck and call.

NOTES

1. This is a well-known quote from Paul Gerhardt. It is actually a verse from an autobiographical poem he wrote. Among other places, it can be accessed at: http://unterkunft.wittenberg.de/e/seiten/personen/gerhardt.html.

2. Henry David Thoreau, *Walden* (New York: Barnes & Noble, 2004), 95–97.

3. Christopher Hibbert, *George III: A Personal History* (London: Penguin Books, 1998), 198.

4. Frances Ridley Havergal, *My King: Daily Thoughts for the King's Children* (New York: Anson D. F. Randolph & Company, u.d.), 12–13.

5. Quoted in V. Raymond Edman, *Out of My Life* (Grand Rapids: Zondervan Publishing House, 1961), 103–106.

6. A. H. Letch in Merrill C. Tenney, ed., *Zondervan Pictorial Encyclopedia of the Bible,* vol. 5 (Grand Rapids: Zondervan Publishing House, 1980), 104.

7. For an excellent analysis of this, see John F. Walvoord and Roy B. Zuck, eds., *The Bible Knowledge Commentary: Old Testament* (Colorado Springs: Victor, 2000), 1361–1364.

8. Quoted in Leslie B. Flynn, *Come Alive with Illustrations* (Grand Rapids: Baker, 1987), 23–24.

9. William Steuart McBirnie, *The Search for the Twelve Apostles* (Wheaton, IL: Tyndale House Publishers, 1977), 172–173.

10. Charles Haddon Spurgeon, *Morning and Evening,* devotion for March 25 (evening). This source is available on many Web sites. For example: http://www.geocities.com/Athens/Forum/1327/spurgeon/seo325.html.

11. C. S. Lewis, quoted by *Christianity Today* in "Word Became Flesh: Quotations to Stir Heart and Mind," compiled by Richard A. Kauffman and posted on December 23, 2004 at http://www.christianitytoday.com/global/printer.html?/ct/2004/012/34.60.html.

12. Walvoord and Zuck, *Bible Knowledge Commentary* (Wheaton, IL: Victor Books, 1985), 1335–1336.

13. Quoted by J. I. Packer in *Knowing God* (Downers Grove, IL.: InterVarsity Press, 1973), 103–104.

14. Eschatology is the study of the future; specifically, the study of what the Bible says.

15. A. W. Tozer, *The Knowledge of the Holy* (New York: Harper & Row Publishers, 1961), 7.

16. Thomas Watson, *Gleanings from Thomas Watson* (Morgan, PA: Soli Deo Gloria Publications, 1995), 86.

17. Some of the older translations insert a comma between Wonderful and Counselor, making two names. But most Bible scholars believe that "Wonderful" is an adjective describing "Counselor."

18. R. B. Zuck, E. H. Merrill, and D. L. Bock, *A Biblical Theology of the Old Testament* (Chicago: Moody Press, 1996), 313.

19. W. W. Wiersbe, *Wiersbe's Expository Outlines on the Old Testament* (Wheaton, IL.: Victor Books, 1993).

20. Spurgeon, *Morning and Evening.*

21. D. Martyn Lloyd-Jones, *Spiritual Depression: Its Causes and Cure* (Grand Rapids: Wm. B. Eerdmans Publishing Company, 1965), foreword and p. 11.

22. For a fuller account of John Marrant's life, see Mark Sidwell, *Free Indeed: Heroes of Black Christian History* (Greenville, SC: Bob Jones University Press, 1958), 9–13.

23. Roland H. Bainton, *Here I Stand: A Life of Martin Luther* (Nashville, TN: Abingdon Press, 1978), 173.

24. Quoted in Gordon MacDonald, *Restoring Your Spiritual Passion* (Nashville, TN: Oliver 25. Peter Cartwright, *The Autobiography of Peter Cartwright* (New York: Abingdon Press, 1956), 164.

26. Eric C. Barrett and David Fisher, eds., *Scientists Who Believe: 21 Tell Their Own Stories* (Chicago: Moody Press, 1984), chapter 1.

27. Francis A. Schaeffer, *He Is There and He Is Not Silent* (Wheaton, IL: Tyndale House Publishers, 1972), 13, 15.

28. Adapted from E. Meyers Harrison, *Blazing the Missionary Trail* (Wheaton, IL: Van Kampen Press, 1949), chapter 1.

29. A strange twist to these words occurred in 1888, when the German philosopher Friedrich Wilhelm Nietzsche, a few weeks before his descent into madness, wrote a sort of autobiography entitled: *Ecce Homo: How One Becomes What One Is.* More recently, the phrase *Ecce Homo* has been used in connection with liberal Christian views regarding homosexuality, especially in modern art exhibits.

30. Quoted in Philip H. Eveson, *Martyn Lloyd-Jones* (Leominster, England: Day One Publications, 2004), 116.

31. Charles Haddon Spurgeon, *The New Park Street Pulpit* (Pasadena, TX: Pilgrim Publications, 1981), sermon number 153, September 27, 1857.

32. Quoted in Michael Reagan, *The Hand of God: Thoughts and Impressions Reflecting the Spirit of the Universe* (Philadelphia: Templeton Foundation Press, 1999), 106.

33. Geoffrey T. Bull, *When Iron Gates Yield* (Chicago: Moody Press, n.d.), passim.

34. Charles E. Watson, *What Smart People Do When Dumb Things Happen at Work* (New York: Barnes and Noble Books, 1999), 218.

35. Y. W. Fullerton, *F. B. Meyer: A Biography* (London: Marshall, Morgan, & Scott, n.d.), 182–183.

36. A. J. Gordon, *The Holy Spirit in Missions* (New York: Fleming H. Revell Co., 1893).

37. Dale Carnegie, *How to Win Friends and Influence People* (New York: Simon and Schuster, 1936), 58.

38. F. A. Schaeffer, *The Complete Works of Francis A. Schaeffer: A Christian Worldview* (Westchester, IL: Crossway Books, 1982, 1996).

39. Watson, *What Smart People Do,* 84.

40. Allen C. Emery, *A Turtle on a Fencepost* (Waco, TX: Word Books, 1979), 27-31.

41. Hamilton Smith, ed., *Gleanings From Thomas Watson: Extracts from the Writings of Thomas Watson* (Morgan, PA: Soli Deo Gloria Publication, 1995), 115–117.

42. Emery, *Turtle,* 53.

43. Kenneth S. Wuest, *Hebrews in the Greek New Testament* (Grand Rapids: Wm. B. Eerdmans Publishing Company, 1951), 215.

44. Amy Carmichael, *Edges of His Ways* (Fort Washington, PA: Christian Literature Crusade, 1998), 7.

45. Elias Bredsdorff, *Hans Christian Andersen* (Copenhagen: Hans Reitzels Forlag, 1987), 63–64.

46. Thomas A. Lambie, *A Bride for His Son* (New York: Loizeaux Brothers, 1957), 25–29.

47. William Evans, *Personal Soul-Winning* (Chicago: Moody Press, 1910), 14.

48. Quoted in V. Raymond Edman, *The Disciplines of Life* (Minneapolis: World Wide Publications, 1948), 78.

49. Robert Fulghum, *Words I Wish I Wrote* (New York: Cliff Street Books, 1997), 105.